Strategic Cost Analysis

Strategic Cost Analysis

Dr. Roger Hussey
Dr. Audra Ong

Strategic Cost Analysis
Copyright © Business Expert Press, LLC, 2012.

First published in 2012 by
Business Expert Press, LLC
222 East 46th Street, New York, NY 10017
www.businessexpertpress.com

ISBN-13: 978-1-60649-239-0 (paperback)
ISBN-13: 978-1-60649-240-6 (e-book)
DOI 10.4128/9781606492406

A publication in the Business Expert Press Managerial Accounting collection

Collection ISSN: 2152-7113 (print)
Collection ISSN: 2152-7121 (electronic)

Cover design by Jonathan Pennell
Interior design by Scribe Inc.

First edition: January 2012

10 9 8 7 6 5 4 3 2 1

Printed in the United States of America.

Abstract

Increasing business competition is compelling managers not only to develop realistic and achievable strategies but also to analyze goals in financial terms and to evaluate performance. Managers will need to know the key methods and techniques of strategic cost analysis no matter which sectors they are in – be it manufacturing, service, or the nonprofit sector. The interaction of the organization's activities, the influences of the external world, and the responsibilities of managers need to be captured in financial terms to enable managers to plan, control, and make decisions.

Sales managers, production managers, HR managers, among others, are recipients of financial information that they are expected to understand. They need to appreciate the impact of their decisions on costs, selling prices, investment decisions, and profit. They must be able to analyze, communicate, and act on financial information to be a valuable member of the management team.

This text explains in simple language the methods and techniques of cost analysis that can be applied strategically at any level in an organization. Busy managers will find that the cost information provided will help them plan and control the activities for which they are responsible and also make strategic decisions in the most effective way. Whether you are in a manufacturing or service organization, the book will help you to answer the four questions:

- What did it cost?
- What should it have cost?
- How can we improve?
- What is our next strategic move?

No prior knowledge of accounting or statistics is required. The book defines all key terms and emphasizes the essential knowledge of analyzing cost in a strategic context.

Keywords

strategic cost, cost competencies, job costing, service costing, variance analysis, CVP analysis, value chain analysis, balanced scorecard.

Contents

Preface

In every business, the owners and managers need to know what their product or service costs to deliver and what they can sell it for. They want to make strategic decisions that maximize their profits, and they require information to do this. Even not-for-profit businesses have a service or product that they wish to offer but are constrained by the funding they receive from grants, donations, and bequests.

The simple truth is that you cannot decide what to do unless you know the cost. This link between cost information and strategy has always been present, possibly in an unsophisticated and informal manner. Increasing competiveness and the contributions made by academics, consultants, and practicing business people have made that link explicit. The conclusion is that strategic decisions cannot be successfully made unless you understand cost information.

Strategic Cost Analysis explains the tools that managers need. It examines the different methods of calculating cost, techniques for controlling and monitoring costs, and ways to integrate cost data and strategy into every aspect of the organization. The thrust of the book is to help managers understand and conduct strategic cost analysis so their own performance is improved and they make a substantial contribution to the organization for which they work.

Chapters 1 and 2 discuss the characteristics of organizations and the influence these have on the type of cost information systems that are developed. The different approaches for identifying and classifying costs are explained, and the methods for ascertaining the cost of products, processes, services, activities, and organizations are demonstrated.

The desire to seek improvements is covered in chapters 3 and 4. The different approaches to planning short-term and long-term costs and a full description of the procedures are discussed. Chapter 3 explains cost planning, and we provide comprehensive guidance on the monitoring and control of costs in chapter 4. The emphasis in these chapters is the integration of cost information and strategy formulation and appraisal.

Decision-making techniques are the subject of chapter 5. We explain the behavior of costs where there is fluctuating activity and demonstrate cost techniques to analyze data so you can make an informed choice. Solutions to strategic questions, such as what level of activity is needed to break even, whether a product line should be dropped, and how special orders should be priced, are given.

The final chapter of the book draws together the subjects in earlier chapters to demonstrate strategic cost analysis in action. We discuss how you determine your strategic positioning, reduce costs, evaluate your performance, and find ways of improving it. As with the earlier chapters, the emphasis is the use of cost information by managers so they can contribute to the success of an organization's strategy.

CHAPTER 1

Cost and Strategy

About This Chapter

The essence of a successful organization is the ability to plan and control costs and to have the information to make viable financial decisions. To carry out these activities, managers need data that are relevant to their responsibilities and are received in sufficient time to take action. They also need to understand the terms and definitions used in relation to the costs of various activities and feel confident in engaging, manipulating, and analyzing cost information.

To meet managers' needs for cost information, a significant part of management accounting is concerned with cost accounting, which is based on collecting and analyzing both financial and quantitative data. Traditionally, cost accounting concentrated on specific, detailed historic costs over a short time period. Increasingly, cost accounting is becoming future-oriented and more concerned with internal and external costs. The time frame for strategic cost accounting has become elongated, and attention is paid as much to the *"why"* of a situation as to the *"what."* Costing has become not just a method of data collection but an important indicator of how to better manage the organization in pursuit of its strategy.

Key Definition

Strategic cost analysis helps companies identify, analyze, and use strategically important resources for continuing success.[1]

Strategic cost analysis (SCA) focuses on an organization's various activities, identifies the reasons for their costs, and financially evaluates strategies for creating a sustainable competitive advantage. The technique provides organizations with the total costs and revenues of strategic decisions. This requires creative thinking, and managers need to identify and solve problems from an integrative and cross-functional viewpoint.

Examples of SCA include the following:

- Deciding on product mixes and production volumes
- Outsourcing decisions
- Cost reductions
- Investment and profit growth in different markets
- Responses to suppliers' and competitors' activities
- Changes in consumer demand

In this chapter we explain the four key questions that, as a manager, you will need the answers to no matter which type of organization you work for. We consider the different types of organizations and how the nature of their activities influence cost methods and techniques. We also explain your need for different forms of cost information to plan, control, and make decisions. The penultimate section explains the process of strategic cost analysis and completes the chapter by explaining the relationship between financial and management accounting.

Before you continue with the chapter, we wish to emphasize that strategic cost accounting is entirely a voluntary practice carried out by organizations. There are no rules or regulations that indicate how strategic cost accounting should be conducted. It is entirely the responsibility of management to determine their needs. If the cost information generated is of no value to managers, it should be abandoned.

As strategic costing systems are designed to satisfy the needs of managers within an organization, the application and terminology of specific costing methods and techniques may develop within the culture of that organization and not correspond exactly with the terms commonly used in the literature. As long as you understand the concepts and the principles, this should cause no problems.

The Four Key Questions

What Did It Cost and Why?

This is possibly the most frequent question asked by managers and where the answers given by accountants are usually misunderstood. The term "cost" is slippery and defies one simple definition. It is therefore helpful to describe and classify the term in a variety of ways. Precision can first be given to the question by defining what is meant by "it," which is known as the cost object.

A broad definition of a cost object is anything for which cost data are required. This can refer to labor, materials, products, services, organizational subdivisions such as departments or divisions of a company, or specific activities. The term is also used to refer to a measure of organizational output, and we discuss the various types of output later in the chapter.

As well as defining the "it" for which you require cost data, you will also need to specify the nature of the cost. Are you only interested in the cost of material used in manufacturing a product, or do you also need to know the cost of the machine time taken in manufacturing? There are various bases of classification and, importantly, as we will see in chapter 2, the amount of "cost" for a particular unit of production or service can change depending on the level of activity.

The more precise you are in referring to the nature of the cost, the better your analysis of cost data is. You want to know not only what a particular cost is but how you can analyze the data effectively to enhance your managerial performance.

What Should It Have Cost?

This question is about setting standards and conducting comparisons. The present cost can be compared to the following:

- *Previous costs for the same activity*. This will show whether we did better or worse than for a prior period of time. Unfortunately, all the errors and deficiencies in incurring the previous cost will obscure whether performance has improved.

- *Costs for alternative courses of action.* This could range from outsourcing or switching to different products or processes.
- *Planned costs.* These will involve the careful assessment of predetermined costs for a specific period of time.
- *Costs of external organizations.* This information may be difficult to acquire, but strategic competitiveness should be a part of an organization's portfolio.

In chapter 3 we explain standard setting, and you will probably find that you will be involved in this activity in the organization where you work. There may be a system of standard costing or of budgetary control or both. Planning future costs is a major part of these costing techniques.

How Can We Improve?

Improvement entails changes in performance levels, which involves determining appropriate measures for the particular activity and monitoring changes in performance. Establishing appropriate measures usually presents problems, and a variety of solutions can be employed. At the organizational level, financial measures such as profit as a percentage of the investment in the company may be used. Where information is available, similar measures can be made at the divisional level. As a manager, you have a certain area of responsibility, and your focus is on how you manage the performance of your responsibility area and how you can improve it.

Cost accounting is an internal information system used by managers, and usually performance measures are related to costs incurred and can be compared to one of the aspects discussed in the previous section. You need to be able to analyze your actual performance compared to that expected and make decisions about improvements. This material is covered in both chapter 4 and chapter 5.

What Is Our Next Strategic Move?

Whatever your responsibility level in an organization, your performance is aligned to corporate strategy, and you may be involved in determining corporate strategy. In the context of strategic cost analysis, what is your contribution? In a recent survey of 500 market leaders, three distinct strategies to be used by top performers in 2012 were identified.[2] One of these was cost and complexity reduction to make operations more flexible, leaner, and more accessible to customers. Whether you are working in a service company, a manufacturing company, or some form of public organization, the benefits of cost and complexity reduction can decrease the financial outlay in bringing the product or service to the customer.

You will have the challenge of attempting to introduce cost and complexity reduction so that the organization, and your part of it, is highly responsive to customer, local, and global business conditions and economic events. In chapter 6 we explain how certain techniques of strategic cost analysis can help you to achieve this

Making the Fit

We observed earlier that management accounting and cost accounting are internal systems unfettered by regulations. Managers in the organization decide the types of cost information they require. This structuring of the system by managers is known as contingency theory, which postulates that organizational structures and systems are a function of environmental and firm-specific factors.[3]

If you work in a large organization, you will find that the management accountant is usually responsible for providing cost data analyzed in a particular way. In a smaller organization you may find that you have to collect the cost information. Whatever the size of the organization, the following factors generally shape the costing system:

- The type of organization
- The output from the activity
- The purposes for which the cost information is required

These factors determine the techniques selected when presenting information in a form that can be analyzed to support and monitor strategic decisions.

The Type of Organization

Cost accounting is practiced in hospitals, banks, universities, and manufacturing companies and by plumbers, electricians, landscape gardeners, charities, and any other organization or individuals who need to know the financial consequences of the activities they undertake or plan to undertake. In many instances, managers want to know the cost of a specific output from an activity, as that forms the basis of the price to be charged. In nonprofit organizations, the total amount of funds available for a period of time or a specific range of activities are predetermined. Thus managers must ensure that the costs for which they are individually responsible fall within those limitations. Strategies will have financial boundaries set on them by external factors, such as donations and government grants.

You should bear in mind that organizations have very different activities. Some will be manufacturers with substantial production facilities. Others will be merchandising companies that do no manufacturing but buy in their goods and sell them at a profit. A very large sector of the economy is service organizations and, within this category, you have a great diversity ranging from financial institutions to hospitals, hotels, airlines, and others. They all have a need for cost information, but the type of organization will determine the nature of information the managers require.

As well as calculating the costs for specific outputs, an organization may wish to know the cost of operating one identifiable part of the organization. For example, an engineering organization may wish to know the monthly cost of running a maintenance department; a municipality may wish to know the cost of operating a garbage collection; a publishing firm, the cost of their art department. These are examples of cost centers or pools, which are identifiable parts of an organization for which costs can be collected and analyzed.

Organizational Constituents

Managers need cost information to plan, monitor, and control the organization's performance. But there are many external groups that have an interest in an organization's performance, and their expectations may influence the nature of the cost information and the assessment of performance. These stakeholders may have differing objectives that influence their assessment of the organization's performance. These influences also affect strategy choices, and cost analysis is needed to assess the financial constraints.

Commercial organizations quoted on a stock exchange have investors who are conscious of the "market" expectations for profit. All organizations have employees who will be concerned with job security and career progression. Customers, suppliers, and even society have expectations and vested interests in the organizations. Managers will be aware of these when reporting their key performance indicators.

The potential impact of external expectations on organizational financial performance was investigated in a project that examined the Central Bank of Norway and a large university hospital in the same country.[4] The research assessed society's expectations of the financial performance of each and the impact on the disclosure of financial results as revealed by their budgeted achievements.

The managers responsible for the approval of budgets in the Bank were aware that society expected that the Bank would operate within its budget. The managers, therefore, set a budget at a high enough level to ensure that at the year's end there would be no spending in excess of the budgeted amount.

The hospital's mission was service to the community, and their responsibility, as seen by the community, was to treat as many patients as necessary, even if that meant exceeding the budget. With changes in patients' treatments and increases in activity, a budget overspend was regarded as evidence that the hospital required greater funding to satisfy the expectations of the community.

This unusual but interesting example demonstrates that strategic cost accounting is framed by the expectations of various groups and is closely connected to human behavior. When using strategic cost accounting, you must therefore be alert to which group is the main financer of the organization and which groups are the main beneficiaries. These are frequently different groups.

Output From Activities

Organizations produce an output, which may be readily identifiable, or a performance measure can be devised. This is sometimes referred to as a *cost object*, as defined earlier, although the term *cost unit* may be used to refer to one single measure of output, whether this is a product such as a bottle of detergent or a service such as a night in a hotel.

A specific definition of a cost unit is a quantitative unit of the product or service to which costs are allocated. In Europe the term "cost unit" is frequently used to refer to one measure of output, although cost object is commonly used in North America. In this book we will use the term "cost unit" where it is clear that we are referring to one unit of output. You should find out the term used in your company and the measure of output to which it refers.

The nature of the output will determine the cost object. For example, a large accounting firm carrying out audits may consider the cost object is related to a certain client: the audit job that the firm performs. A garage may also consider its cost object as a repair job insofar as it does a specific task for an identified client. A construction company building a new hospital will consider this a cost object, although it may take several years to complete.

Other organizations may have output that is continuous. A paint manufacturer will not produce a can of paint specific for one customer but will produce daily hundreds or thousands of cans of paint that may be purchased by anyone. The paint manufacturer will therefore want to know the cost of one can of paint. Service companies may also offer an output that is (to all intent and purpose) continuous, although there may be an identified customer. Usually that output is not tangible, and a performance measure must be devised that is useful to the company. For example, a hotel may want to know the cost of an occupied room for one night.

An organization such as a recreation center may offer clients a range of pursuits such as swimming, volleyball, or badminton. The cost information they will most likely collect is the cost per hour or day for offering each of the different activities. Other organizations that offer clients a standard service, such as a beauty salon, may wish to know the average cost of offering each of the standard services.

Managerial Information Needs

In a small business, the owner may be the only "manager." The cost system is likely to be rudimentary and informal. The owner is likely to make all the decisions, and performance measure is of the entire business and not different parts of it. The relationship between cost analysis and strategy is likely to be very strong with only one person using the financial information to make unilateral decisions. However, it is unlikely to be sophisticated.

As a business grows, delegation of decision-making takes place. Managers need to receive quantitative and financial data on which to base their decisions. As a manager, you wish to know the cost of the products or services for which you are responsible or the costs of operating your specific area.

To assist in identifying costs that are the responsibilities of specific managers, larger organizations are divided into various functional areas or centers. If you are the manager of a responsibility center, you normally participate in the objectives of that center, and you are given some discretion on their achievement. The cost data that you receive assist you in analyzing your performance.

The centers that you find in an organization are adapted to the nature and purpose of the organization but usually fall under one of the following four categories:

- *Cost centers (CCs)* to which costs are attributed but not revenues or capital. A cost center does not generate external revenue. For example, in a manufacturing organization, the maintenance department or security would be a cost center. For a magazine publisher, the section providing artwork could be a cost center.
- *Revenue centers (RCs)* to which revenues are attributed but not costs or capital. The costs of running the revenue center itself are allocated and monitored to the center but not the costs of generating products or services.
- *Profit centers (PCs)* to which costs and revenues are attributed but not capital. This could be a shop in a chain of retailers or a division of a large company.
- *Investment centers (ICs)* to which costs, revenues, and capital are attributed. This is possibly the largest type of responsibility center, as the manager will be responsible for resource funding (capital) decisions.

The Process of Strategic Cost Analysis

Some view strategic cost analysis as a collection of new topics—the value chain, a balanced scorecard, and added economic value, among others—but it is much more than that. It is a different way of viewing cost management.[5] Strategic cost analysis is about helping organizations succeed, and this means employing different cost management techniques in different circumstances.

Although we have explained in this chapter that traditional costing as a subject is an internal process shaped by the needs of the organization and the managers within it, strategic cost analysis is externally as well as internally focused. It employs past data to illuminate future choices. In a study examining the use of cost information for strategic purposes, Al-Hazmi concluded that "cost information is being used in management thinking to support strategic development in meeting competitive pressures and in restructuring and the reconfiguration of business strategy."[6]

Attempts have been made to identify and classify the various techniques that can be used in strategic management accounting. Cadez[7] drew together and added to previous contributions to construct a taxonomy of 16 techniques sorted into 5 categories, with strategic costing falling under the strategic decision-making category. The analysis provides a useful overview for identifying techniques and their categories. It also emphasizes the importance of strategic cost accounting for the short-term and long-term management of an organization. However, it tends to delineate the techniques too distinctly without reflecting their integration and how the dynamism of the subject and the use by companies generate new and fresh practices.

You may be working in an organization that has a traditional costing system mainly concerned with collecting data from past production processes. The question arises as to how you convert that system so you can achieve the benefits that strategic cost accounting offers. It is about not just reading the methods and techniques that are explained but changing your mind-set. The following three steps are advised:[8]

1. Audit both your existing and planned cost initiatives to ensure that the proposed changes improve the organization's strategic cost management. The advice given in this book will help you with this stage.

2. Extend the scope of internal costing beyond the walls of the factory. We would emphasize that whether you are in a manufacturing, service, or public organization you need to investigate the departments and activities that would be managed more successfully with strategic cost accounting.

3. Extend the cost management program beyond the boundaries of the firm. In other words, strategic cost accounting also includes the external environment.

We would add one final step. Focus on the future in your strategic cost analysis, as well as learn from the past.

The Five Forces Model

Possibly the best-known work on strategy is Porter's[9] Five Forces model. His "activity-based view" has made an immense contribution to thinking on strategy, and a full appreciation of the impact of his work is excellently explained by Sheehan and Foss.[10] In this section we will focus on Porter's contention that the following competitive forces affect a company's profits:

1. The threat of new entrants into an industry or market served by a specific company
2. The bargaining power of suppliers
3. The bargaining power of the consumer
4. The threat of substitute products or services
5. The intensity of rivalry among existing firms

Porter's thesis is that, if a company is to be successful, it must adopt a strategy that combats these forces better than the strategy developed by its rivals. To do this, a company has a choice of three strategies: cost leadership, product differentiation, and focus or niche. We will look at the first two, as Porter argues that a company must choose either of the following:

• Cost leadership, where the organization can offer the market products or services at a low cost compared to competitors

- Product differentiation, where the organization's products or services are considered by customers as superior to that of competitors, and therefore a premium price for the goods or services can be demanded

Cost leadership—that is, the lowest delivered cost to a customer—gives an organization several advantages over its competitors. One advantage is that the impact of competition is minimized by allowing the organization to increase profit margins at the prevailing level of industry prices. An organization may also become the price leader because competitors cannot compete where their costs are higher.

Product differentiation allows companies to improve their profit margins by charging higher prices for a product or exempting it from a price-cutting war with its competitors. If the product differentiation has high customer appeal, then retailers will wish to deal in the product.

One argument against cost leadership is that it is not a competitive strategy because customers buy a product not on the basis of a firm's cost structure but on the basis of their own preferences and priorities, although they may be influenced by price. A cost leadership strategy must involve price cutting to attract the mass market. Additionally, if an organization is in the position where it does not already have a low cost structure, it can risk a price war, as it may not survive it.

Once the corporate-level strategy has been decided, managers must implement it at the business or operational level. This will require planning, making decisions, and controlling activities to achieve the desired strategy. Managers need cost accounting to perform these functions.

Identifying Costs

You should not interpret the previous discussion on cost leadership as meaning that all companies must pursue cost reductions regardless. Cost leaders compete on low price, whereas differentiators focus on innovation, features, customer service, or other means to attract customers who are willing to pay a premium price. You should not confuse good cost management because companies have different strategies. Strategic cost analysis means that they will have different performance measures and different planning, control, and decision-making methods. Companies use cost management to pursue their strategies effectively.

You may have heard the phrase "different costs for different purposes." The implication of this is that each management purpose or objective requires specific cost identification and will require appropriate costing methods and techniques. Because of his or her specific skills and experience, the accountant in the organization will play a prominent role in collecting the cost data and assisting in its analysis. But the accountant is only one part of the integrated management team responsible for strategy.

Each manager is responsible for the performance of his or her own center. To discharge this responsibility effectively and efficiently, you must have a full understanding of what is meant by cost and of the techniques you can use to analyze cost data and evaluate your performance. The purpose of a costing system is to "help guide management in making decisions on how to best use these limited resources strategically."[11]

Comparing With Plans

By comparing actual performance with predetermined performance, management can make assessments and conduct investigations to remedy deficiencies and to promote good practices. The comparison gives both control and the information to make decisions. Comparing with plans is therefore part of a control loop.

With the control loop, the plans should lead to action. The action is then measured and the actual performance compared with the plans. If there are differences, an investigation must be conducted and a decision made. This may be to review the plans, as they were unsatisfactory, or to concentrate on improving the actual performance. At every stage in the control loop, strategic cost analysis will be required.

The assumptions and decisions about future activity levels are the basis of the plans. An organization may be in an environment where activity levels have a certain degree of predictability either because of constrained capacity of the organization or because of the stability of the marketplace.

Where the activity levels are judged to be reasonably consistent, the organization may determine that its priority is planning and controlling the actual costs of material and labor. Alternatively, and often additionally, it will pay attention to period costs—that is, those costs associated with a period of time rather than actual activity levels, such as rent, insurance, salaries, or administrative costs.

In chapters 4 and 5, we explain the use of standard costing for the direct materials and labor costs incurred in providing a product or service. We also describe the application of budgetary control for the planning and monitoring of period costs. In addition, we demonstrate the use of static and flexible budgets to allow for changes in activity levels.

Organizations that experience a turbulent environment and uncertainty in planning will need to examine various alternative courses of action and have the flexibility to change to meet fresh challenges. A well-constructed and well-implemented strategic cost analysis system will allow them to do this.

Seeking Improvements

By comparing your actual performance against plans, you can assess your managerial abilities. The next stage is to know how you can improve your performance. A range of techniques have been developed and are still being generated to support managers in their quest for improved performance.

In chapter 6 we explain the application of these techniques. You will find that each technique has its strong supporters and also its critics. As a manager you must remember that strategic cost analysis is about using the techniques that best help you and your organization develop and achieve a competitive strategy. You select the technique that best fits the type of organization, the activities it undertakes, and your own responsibilities. It is there to serve you!

Strategic cost analysis is about gearing your company's performance to the external economics and the internal dynamics. You must be able to think strategically about the long-run impact of short-term cost changes and use your knowledge and skills to minimize cost pressures on the organizational strategy.

You will experience the daily pressures to cope with internal rising costs, but you must also recognize that there may be uneven cost changes with your competitors. Small, short-term disparities can result in long-term shifts in your cost competitiveness and any cost advantage you enjoy.

Performance Measurement

What to Measure

If you are the manager, you will have some autonomy on how you run the area for which you are responsible. The metrics used to assess how you have performed as a manager are normally based on some form of comparison of your actual costs, revenues, or profits against a predetermined amount. These are usually the financial components of the agreed strategy.

If you manage a cost center, you may demonstrate improved performance by maintaining the quality of the activity but reducing the costs or improving the quality while maintaining the cost level. There may even be circumstances where you are able to reduce cost levels and simultaneously improve quality.

If you are managing a profit center, the absolute amount of profit will be important, but this may also be expressed as a percentage of your sales figure or as a percentage return on the resources you employ. These, and similar, percentage comparisons are valuable for tracing performance over time and for comparing to profit centers both within and external to the organization.

Any type of center has performance measurement issues. With cost centers, there is frequently the assumption held by senior management and the managers of other centers that its costs are too high. The manager of a cost center can always attempt to reduce costs, but this may lead to a reduction in services. For example, a maintenance department will take longer to respond with its services because employee numbers have been reduced. A cleaning department may clean certain areas on alternate days instead of daily.

To overcome these issues, some organizations will make an internal charge for the use of a cost center. For example, a printing department may start charging for leaflets and brochures it produces for other departments. The user departments may then decide to try for external competitive quotes and, if they choose this and accept them, this will reduce the "income" of the print department. The record keeping needed to make the internal charges will be an additional cost.

Sometimes a strategic decision is made to change a cost center into a profit center to avoid these problems. It is not always successful and can result in the "failure of the internal market."[12] This is where other departments use outside resources for their needs instead of the internal provider. If the cost center is a vital internal resource, it cannot be allowed to fail. It will be the responsibility of managers to ensure that the cost levels are consistent with the level of service provided.

The purpose and role of a center is pivotal to the collection and analysis of cost data. Although practices within one country will have similarities, you should be aware that if you have international responsibilities, you may encounter significant differences. A recent comparison of Germany and the United States concluded that there were differences in practices concerning classification of costs, measures to use when considering changes in costs, and the size and scope of the cost center and managerial responsibility.[13]

You Get What You Measure

Cost systems affect behavior in the workplace because they either explicitly or implicitly recognize and reward the performance of managers. Bonuses, career progression, and even slaps on the back and congratulatory words are likely to direct a manager's efforts and behavior. In all probability, the direction followed will be what is being measured and rewarded. This can be in conflict with what is required to achieve organizational strategy.

You can imagine that if the performance of a sales person is measured on the number of new customers obtained, there will be a tendency to concentrate on that and ignore maintaining a good relationship with existing customers. If employees are paid a bonus on the volume of work they achieve in a certain time, there may be a lack of attention to quality unless that is also measured in some way.

In an attempt to measure the performance required from employees, some companies construct an array of key performance indicators (KPIs). The intention of these is to minimize attention being focused on just one aspect of performance to the detriment of other important aspects. But even here, care needs to be taken, and the SMART criteria technique has been advocated.[14] This requires that a KPI must satisfy these five criteria: specific, measurable, attainable, relevant, and time bound. Hursman emphasizes that "relevant" means relevant to the employee and not just the company.

Any KPI system will undoubtedly include financial information, and in chapters 3 and 4 we explain the role of standard costing and budgetary control in establishing plans and providing feedback to allow managers to monitor and control performance. Both researchers and practitioners have identified the close relationship between behavior and the budgetary control systems. These can take many forms.

Budgets are the financial aspect of strategy, and decisions are being made about the amount and type of resources that managers will have to discharge in their work responsibilities. Understandably, managers will be inclined to argue for the maximum amount of resources, as this will make their job easier. The issue of budget "padding" is a common problem. Also, the size of a budget for which a manager has responsibility will sometimes be regarded as a sign by others of their eminence or otherwise in the organization.

In monitoring performance against the budget, managers can be tempted to ensure that the budget amount is completely spent; otherwise there is a fear that the budget will be reduced in the following financial period. Managers may also be constrained from demonstrating any initiatives if there is not scope in the budget to allow it.

The problems of unwanted behaviors should not be overemphasized, but as a manager, you should be aware of them. Costing is not just about numbers. It is about the activities of people and their endeavors to use the resources for which they have a responsibility to achieve an agreed strategic goal.

Financial and Managerial Accounting

We complete this chapter with a discussion of the relationship between financial and management accounting. Most textbooks treat these separately, but they are intertwined; this should be remembered when reading subsequent chapters.

The dominant characteristics of managerial accounting are that it is intended for an internal audience and is a voluntary system implemented by an organization to meet its own needs.

Strategic cost accounting can be considered a subset of managerial accounting, although it is difficult to delineate the boundaries. As with managerial accounting, the purpose of cost accounting is to collect, collate, and communicate information to managers for planning, control, and decision making.

The dominant characteristics of financial accounting are that it is intended to provide information for external audiences and is regulated. Even very small businesses must provide information to the tax authorities, and larger companies are regulated by accounting standards and may additionally be listed on a stock exchange by those regulations.

The two forms of accounting, in many organizations, extract their data from a common set of financial records. The main purpose of these records is to produce data for financial accounting. Although the records may be suitably flexible to extract appropriate cost data, the core concepts of financial accounting tend to be pervasive—for example, determining which transactions are deemed as *revenue expenses* and counted as costs in the current financial period and which transactions are *capital expenses* and appear on the organization's balance sheet.

The relationship of the two systems is most visible in the following:

1. Listed companies in North America are required to produce interim financial statements quarterly and in the UK biannually. Usually the cost data for these periods must be aligned to the financial disclosures. It would be imprudent for a company to disclose quarterly or biannual financial information that did not relate to the cost information available internally and did not produce information that enabled reasonable predictions of the annual financial results.

2. In the next chapter, we will consider process costing. Most textbooks concentrate on the use of this method for finding the cost of finished inventory and work in process. This is to meet financial disclosure needs, and we will explore in greater detail the strategic costing requirements of this method.

3. Cost accounting, as with financial accounting, uses the "accruals" concept of accounting for transactions. This means that transactions are recognized when they take place and not when cash is received or paid, although the events may be simultaneous, such as when you pay at the checkout of a supermarket. Often transactions are

complex, and accounting standards set out the requirements for these transactions to be recognized for financial accounting purposes, but this also frames the cost for strategic cost purposes.

4. The method of determining the financial measurement of a transaction is set by accounting standards and is recorded on that basis. These data will also be used in determining the strategic costs.

Financial accounting requirements are complex and sometimes imperfect. We do not wish to overemphasize the influence of these requirements on strategic cost accounting, but it is important that you are aware that sometimes the reasons for unresolved issues may lie with financial accounting requirements and not the methods and techniques of strategic cost accounting.

Conclusions

In this introductory chapter, you should have gained insights into the relationship between an organization's costing system and its strategic plans. All organizations have limited resources that must be used in providing services and products in a competitive environment, and as a manager you contribute to this effort. To do so, you require cost information, and we have explained how you can direct your attention to the cost information you need and how that information will be shaped by several factors.

Cost is a slippery term, so you need to

- be specific on what is being costed,
- know what the cost should be,
- understand how performance can be improved,
- set the information within the organization's strategy.

There are no regulations that require organizations to have costing systems. It is purely a voluntary activity designed to assist managers in

- planning their activities,
- controlling performance against the plans,
- making decisions about alternative courses of action.

To do this, managers need cost information, but that information must meet the needs of the organization and that of individual managers. Although principles and concepts are explained and discussed in this book, organizations will "customize" them. The following factors influence the shape of the costing system:

- The type of organization that will include such considerations as size, structure, and purpose
- The organizational constituents, who may be investors, shareholders, the local community, and society at large
- The output from the activities that may be tangible manufactured goods, services, or even professional advice
- The information needs of the manager, which will depend on the manager's role and responsibilities

The process of strategic costing uses many different techniques that are discussed in subsequent chapters. But strategic costing is not about an array of various methods and techniques but about how to help organizations succeed. The process of strategic costing should therefore

- build on the core competencies of the organization,
- identify the costs that are relevant to its needs,
- generate valuable comparisons with its plans,
- support the search for improved performance.

The following chapters will explain the purposes, strengths, and weaknesses of various costing techniques and guide managers in selecting those that are most valuable in their search for a strategic solution.

CHAPTER 2

Cost Concepts and Methods

About This Chapter

In this chapter, we address the question raised in chapter 1: "What did it cost?" As observed in the previous chapter, "cost" is a slippery term. You will find that the more precisely you identify the cost you are interested in, the more useful will be the information for analysis. You may be seeking the cost of materials used in production for a certain period of time, the cost of conducting a laser surgery operation, the cost of making a part of a product compared to buying in, or the cost of being the defense team in a major fraud trial.

This range of activities leads us to the question of what is being "costed." In other words, you want to know the cost of conducting the laser operation or the cost of making one can of paint. These are all very different activities, and we therefore need some system of classifying "costs" into useful categories. We also need to recognize that these very different activities will require different methods to assemble our costs. In this chapter, we commence by considering different methods of classifying costs, based on both the nature of the cost and the way it accumulates.

The largest part of this chapter explains how you calculate the *total* cost of a particular product or activity. There are two primary methods for calculating the total cost of a product or service: full costing and activity-based costing. How each of these two methods is applied will depend on whether you are working for an organization that has a specific order of operations or one that has continuous operations. The importance of the difference in these operations is discussed later.

You will appreciate that this chapter explains concepts and methods individually. In a large organization, there may be both production and service activities of varying natures. Not only is an array of costing methods and techniques used, but also the classification of costs is determined by the nature of those specific activities.

The Nature of Costs

Cost Classification

Classifications are used in all walks of life. For example, you can take a group of people and classify them by gender, age, and weight. Depending on your purposes, you may then want to draw up subclassifications such as a subgroup of males over the age of 50 years and weighing less than 85 kilograms.

The same principles are used when we are classifying "cost." The classification we use will be determined by the reason for requiring the information. For example, a purchasing manager may be interested in the cost of raw materials; a sales manager in the costs of running the sales department; the production manager in the total cost in one unit of production; and the security manager in the hourly cost of offering 24-hour security. In Table 2.1, we illustrate the basic types of cost classification, a brief explanation of that classification, and in the third column some examples.

You will note that these broad classifications can be merged to provide a more useful description of the type of cost. For example, raw materials can usually be identified with a cost object, which means that they are direct costs, and as such, they are variable. In other words, the more cost units you make the greater, in total, will be the cost of raw materials.

In this chapter we conduct a thorough examination of direct and indirect costs. This enables us to explain how we can calculate the total cost of a particular service or product. Note that costs can also be classified as either controllable or uncontrollable depending on whether the manager has discretion to control the costs. For example, if an organization has the authority to hire part-time or temporary staff when needed, then these wages are controllable costs. For budgetary planning and control purposes, standard costs are compared with actual costs in order to calculate variances. Budgets and variance analysis are discussed in chapter 4. Not only do managers find that the classification of fixed and variable costs are extremely useful in decision making, but they need to understand the concept of opportunity costs and sunk costs. These are explored further under relevant costing or incremental analysis in chapter 5.

Table 2.1. Cost Classification

Classification	Explanation	Examples
Nature	The main headings are materials, labor, and overheads.	Raw materials, work in process, supervisory staff, depreciation, insurance
Function	The purpose of the cost, which is usually aligned to cost or profit centers.	Administration costs, production costs, distribution costs
Product costs	These are costs that can be directly identified with a particular product or service.	Raw materials or bought-in parts in manufacturing, costs of staff in an accounting or law firm
Period costs	These are costs that are related to a financial period.	Insurance for the buildings, salaries of administration staff
Direct costs	These are costs that can be identified with a specific cost object that is a particular product, department, or other cost object.	Raw materials used in production and labor where it can be traced to that particular activity
Indirect costs (overheads)	These cannot be identified with an individual cost object but may be organization wide.	Supervisor salaries, heating in the buildings, telephone costs
Variable costs	This is a behavioral classification, and these costs change in total as activity changes.	Materials used in making the cost object
Fixed costs	This is a behavioral classification and refers to those costs that stay the same in total regardless of changes in levels of activity.	Rent, insurance
Mixed cost	A semivariable cost that varies with volume but not in proportion to volume.	Telephone bills that include a fixed charge for basic service plus a variable charge for long-distance calls

Although cost classifications are often explained in a manufacturing context, this is only for simplicity. Managers in all types of organizations, including financial services, "need to be cognizant of the myriad of definitions that surround the word cost."[1]

Direct Costs

In a manufacturing organization, materials that can be identified directly with the product are likely to be significant. The increasing use of mechanization and robotics has, in some industries, reduced the amount of direct labor required. But be cautious: In some industries, where skilled labor is an essential part of the manufacturing process, the cost can be high. Generally, in service industries direct labor will be high and material low or even insignificant. An accounting firm doing a major audit will have high direct labor costs but practically zero direct material costs.

Direct material costs will normally have the following characteristics:

- *Detectable.* This will often mean that they are visible, although with some direct materials, such as gases, this may not be the case and special equipment may be needed to detect them.
- *Measurable.* This can be by weight, volume, time, or another appropriate method.
- *Relatively valuable.* Some costs are of small value, and it is not useful to maintain records to calculate the costs to a specific cost object. For example, in manufacturing, the costs of such items as glues, thread, and screws are so minor that ordinary physical controls are sufficient, such as allowing a certain quantity for a specific level of production.
- *Traceable.* A system must be in operation to be able to record the quantity of materials for the specific product or service.

Calculating the cost of direct materials to specific cost objects can cause difficulties. These fall under two headings: the practical and the price. On a practical basis, good records and work procedures are essential to ensure that materials are correctly received from the suppliers, stored in safe and secure conditions, and only issued when required by production. This usually safeguards the processing of the correct quantity of materials, but the problem of pricing, or determining the costs, remains.

The delivery of materials may take place over a period of time, and this does not necessarily synchronize with the quantities being issued to production. Prices will therefore vary over that period of time due to

- inflation or deflation giving rise to price changes;
- variations in exchange rates if materials are purchased overseas;
- shortages in the supply of materials, leading to price increases;
- temporary reductions due to special offers, discounts, and so on.

There are several methods used for determining the price of the materials issued to production. Of course, the method chosen for issues to production also affects the value of the closing inventory. This amount will be shown on the financial statements, and financial accounting standards determine which methods are acceptable. Most companies will select a method that meets the requirements of the financial accounting standard and also establishes a cost that is useful for management. Whatever method is used, the overriding requirement is that inventory should be valued at less than the cost and the net realizable value (i.e., the amount it could be sold for less the costs of selling).

The cost of direct labor is usually based on the remuneration system used in the company. It is essential that a sound record system is in place to charge the correct cost of labor to the appropriate activity. For example, in a manufacturing organization, piecework tickets or swipe cards may be used to record the times of different types of labor at various stages of the production process on a job. Time sheets are widely used in manufacturing and service industries. For example, employees in accounting or law firms will record their billable hours for each client's job.

Indirect Costs (Overheads)

In addition to those direct costs that can be identified with the production or service activity, there are also indirect costs, which in many organizations are higher than the direct costs. Usually these overheads can be grouped under the following headings:

- Production overheads
- Administration overheads
- Selling overheads

Depending on the nature of the organization's activities, there may also be distribution overheads and research and development overheads. In some organizations, the distribution cost of a particular product can be significant and identified directly with the job. Research costs are usually regarded as overheads but for a large project may be considered direct.

In a service organization, the overheads can be substantial. If you stay in a hotel, the costs of cleaning your room and the complimentary breakfast are insignificant. It is the property tax for the hotel site, the depreciation charge on fixtures, furniture and equipment, lighting and heating, and the hotel staff you see, such as the staff at the front desk. These are the costs of running the hotel.

If we wish to know the total cost of a cost object, we need to ascertain the following:

- Direct material costs
- Direct labor costs
- Overhead costs

Whether we are establishing the costs of building a bridge, manufacturing and installing a computerized system, conducting a surgical operation, or defending a client on a murder charge, there will be records of the direct costs incurred if the amount involved is worth recording.

The critical issue is how we share the total overheads for the organization over the various activities and the cost objects generated within one financial period. You want to know how much it costs you to run your department, repair a car for a client, transport 100 meters of steel over 50 kilometers, or set up an emergency hospital in a disaster area. In some instances, the indirect costs may not be of overwhelming importance, but usually they are.

There are two methods for ascertaining total cost: traditional (full) costing and activity-based costing. Both try to resolve the same problem of sharing overheads over cost objects and activities.

Ascertaining the Total Cost

Full Costing or Absorption Costing

We start this section by stating what we do *not* mean by full costing. In the last few decades, there have been attempts to calculate the full costs of an organization's activities by including social, environmental, and economic costs. The traditional accounting approach is therefore expanded to include costs that make up what is referred to as the triple bottom line, a term introduced by John Elkington.[2]

In our explanations, we restrict the use of the term "full costing," also known as absorption costing or traditional costing, as a cost accounting method designed to identify the material, labor, and overhead costs incurred to provide a product or service. The method was developed in the manufacturing sector and reflects the priorities of production facilities, although the technique is widely used in other sectors. The purpose of the technique is to find the total cost, including overheads, of the cost object.

Full costing seeks to provide answers to two practical problems:

- How to share the total overheads of the organization over the various production cost centers
- How to share the overheads for a particular production cost center over the various products passing through it

Some overheads can be identified directly with a cost center because the activities of that center necessarily incurred the cost, such as the insurance on some highly specialized equipment used only in one department. The second group of overheads cannot be identified with a single cost center, but must be shared over all the cost centers benefiting from them. For example, the costs of cleaning, lighting, heating, insurance, and property tax for an organization need to be charged in some way to each production department. The second step is to charge a share of that department's overhead to each cost object passing through it.

The stages of sharing organizational overheads are summarized as follows:

- Charge those overheads to the department that causes them.
- Share the remaining overheads over the departments by preparing an overhead analysis statement.
- Charge a share of the departmental overhead to each cost object passing through it to give the total production cost of each cost object.

In this chapter, we give an example of using allocation costing both for a company that does work for specific customers and for an organization where there is continuous output. At this point, we give a simple example to demonstrate the stages of sharing organizational overheads. Remember that we are only concerned with indirect costs and not direct materials and direct labor.

Example of Overhead Analysis Statement and Allocation Rate

In this example, we assume that there are just two production departments in the factory, and the production goes first to Department 1 and is completed in Department 2. Table 2.2 shows the characteristics of the company.

Table 2.3 shows the amount of overhead that has been budgeted for the financial period, and how it has been allocated over the two departments. From this very simple example, you can see that of the total overhead of $110,000, Department 1 is allocated with $85,000 and Department 2 is allocated with $25,000. We allocated the rent of the factory on the basis of the area occupied by each department. The salary of the supervisors is more controversial.

We used the number of employees on the basis that it is related to the amount of supervision required. This may not be the case, and the employees in Department 2 may be working as a team with little supervision. However, in the absence of any more information, the basis we used seems reasonable on the data available.

One way you can interpret the departmental overhead is to regard it as the cost of the resources required for that department to carry out its

Table 2.2. Company Characteristics

	Total	Department 1	Department 2
Number of employees	20	15	5
Area (sq. feet)	1,000	800	200

Table 2.3. Overhead Analysis

Factory overhead	Budgeted overhead (thousands of dollars)	Basis of allocation	Department 1 (thousands of dollars)	Department 2 (thousands of dollars)
Rent	40	Area	32	8
Supervisors' salaries	60	Number of employees	45	15
Building insurance	10	Area	8	2
Total	110		85	25

part of the production process. In other words, we calculated the cost of running a department regardless of the level of activity.

We shared the overheads on a basis that is normally used in practice, but we are certain you will agree that it is very arbitrary. In defense of this approach, we argue that it is cost efficient and sensible to use a basis in which we already have the information available without incurring further costs to obtain addition cost data. It could be argued that the approach is reasonable and, by and large, will reflect the departments' uses of the resources.

The overheads for the entire factory have now been "shared," but now we need to charge an appropriate amount to the cost object. We should already have a record of the direct materials and labor required to make the product, and by now adding the share of the overheads, we will know the total production cost of the cost object. Other overheads such as selling, distribution, and administration will be discussed later.

There are several ways we can allocate the relevant portion of the overhead to the cost object. The choice of the allocation rate depends on the nature of the product and the resources we consider are being used. There are three methods you are most likely to find in practice.

The Cost Object

If all the units we produce are homogeneous, such as cans of paint, then we can merely divide the department overheads by the number of units going through that department to give us an average overhead cost per unit. This is added to the direct material and direct labor cost to give the total cost per unit. You will find a worked example of this when we discuss process costing toward the end of this chapter.

Labor Hour Rate

If you consider that the costs of running the department are largely incurred to provide labor to work on the cost objects, then you can use labor hours. In the previous example, the overhead costs for Department 1 were $85,000. If management has determined that 10,000 hours of work is carried out in that time, the overhead labor rate is $85,000 / 10,000 = $8.50 per labor hour. If a cost object required 3 labor hours, then the share of overheads for the object is $8.5 × 3 = $25.50. Note that this is *not* the direct labor cost but the share of overheads cost and is added to the direct costs to give the total production cost.

Machine Hour Rate

You may work in an organization where the production process is highly mechanized in particular departments. If that is the case, then you would charge the overheads to the cost object on the basis of the machine hours incurred. For example, the overhead for Department 2 is $25,000 for a set period of time. Management may have determined that this will provide a capacity of 12,500 machine hours. The machine hour rate is $25,000 / 12,500 = $2.00 per machine hour. If a job were to take 100 machine hours to complete, then the cost of the overhead would be 100 x $2.00 = $200.

There are other methods for allocating overheads, such as a percentage of the labor cost or the material cost. These have the advantage of the information already being available but are prone to fluctuations due to changes in labor rates and material prices.

There are three key facts you need to remember:

- Allocation rates are calculated for each department, and different departments can have a different method of allocation.
- The overhead charge is added to the direct costs to obtain the total production cost.
- A cost object will be charged overheads for every department that it passes through.

Service Centers

So far, we have considered only production cost centers. However, most businesses also have cost centers based in the factory that provide services to other cost centers. Examples of *service cost centers* include departments associated with the production areas, such as maintenance and quality control. We will leave consideration of cost centers such as administration and marketing until later in the chapter.

In a small organization where the services provided are not substantial, the costs may be allocated directly to the production cost centers. In a larger organization, the Overhead Analysis Statement will have columns for the service cost centers, and a share of the factory overheads will be allocated to them. The columns are subtotaled, and the subtotal of the service cost centers are allocated to the production cost centers on a fair but arbitrary basis. A useful article by Meeting and Harvey[3] discusses the various approaches that could be used by health care providers in the United States.

Activity-Based Costing (ABC)

You will have concluded, most likely, from our explanations in the first section that full costing involves considerable arbitrary decision making, and in some circumstances, the nature of the organization's activities and the data available would make it difficult to apply. Observing these problems, academics and consultants commenced investigating alternative methods.

The first explanation of activity-based costing as a valid alternative to full costing appeared in 1987.[4] The authors demonstrated the value of the technique in the manufacturing sector where the proportion of the direct costs was falling, and the indirect costs were increasing in importance. Since that date, the use of the technique has spread with adherents in both the manufacturing and service sectors.

In studying ABC, you should bear in mind that the treatment of direct costs is exactly the same as full costing. It is the way that we treat the overheads. With both methods we are using predetermined overheads. These will be the budgeted total costs for rent, insurance, electricity, power, and other indirect costs.

The purpose of ABC is to ascertain the total cost of a product, service, or activity, but the approach it adopts differs from full costing. Instead of being based on functional departments or responsibility centers, activity-based costing uses the concept of "cost pools." Instead of allocation rates to charge overheads to the products, cost drivers are identified. Let us look at these two main stages separately.

Activity Cost Pools

The main *activities* in the organization are classified into activity centers. These can be defined as a unit of the organization that performs an operation that uses resources. It need not be based on an existing functional department. For example, a hospital spends a significant amount of money on medical supplies. As part of this process, orders have to be placed, and this activity consumes resources.

Cost Drivers

Cost drivers must be identified with each activity cost pool. A cost driver is any factor that causes a change in the cost of an activity or series of activities. Using our hospital example, it could be the number of orders placed for medical supplies. For a medical emergency service, it could be the number of patients admitted. Table 8.4 gives examples of cost pools and drivers

A cost driver rate is then calculated by dividing the costs of the particular cost pool by the unit of activity. In our hospital example, it would be the number of orders placed, or the number of patients admitted in an accident and emergency ward.

The final stage is assigning the costs of the cost pool to the product or service being provided. If the cost driver rate for orders for medical supplies is calculated at $10 per order, and in a financial period 500 orders are placed for supplies for heart patients, the total cost is $5,000.

ABC is a more sophisticated system than full costing and, it is claimed, should provide information about costs that is more comprehensive, reliable, and useful than that provided by full costing. The method incorporates all relevant overheads and generates information that enables managers to make better decisions about the management of those activities and the possibilities of cost reduction.

You may be wondering why every business has not changed to ABC, if it is such a good system. One of the main reasons is the question of cost and the problems associated with organizational change. There is little inducement to undertake the substantial changes required to introduce a new system if the business already produces product costing information that meets their needs. Even if the business is not entirely satisfied with

Table 2.4. Examples of Cost Pools and Drivers

Cost pool	Cost driver
Procurement of supplies	Number of orders placed
Machine setup costs	Number of different jobs run
Handling of materials	Quantity or weight of materials handled
Sales administration	Number of customer orders auctioned

its present system, the cost of implementing and managing a new system may seem too burdensome to make it worthwhile.

ABC is probably best suited for organizations where traditional full costing will not provide the information required. This can be due to the complex structure of the organization and the nature of the activities conducted. The method seems to have been particularly beneficial in the service industries and has been implemented by financial institutions and hospitals. There is also some evidence that it is a better method than full costing in the hospitality sector.[5]

The emphasis in ABC on activities has generated an interest in investigating the efficiency in the use of the available capacity. Organizations have committed resources and need to assess the costs and management issues of unused capacity. Capacity cost can be defined as a fixed cost that is essential for the continuing activities of an organization. These costs tend not to vary from month to month, and if capacity is not used fully, there may be opportunities for management to reduce these resources and thus decrease the amount of overhead.

As with full costing, there are weaknesses in ABC not always understood by the nonfinancial manager. This may be particularly evident in ABC where a large component of the cost may be fixed with changing activity levels. ABC, like full costing, relies on the accuracy of the predictions concerning the amount of the overhead and the level of the activity. For example, if an organization calculates that the overhead is $10,000 for a financial period with 1,000 cost drivers, the application rate will be $10 per driver. However, if the actual activity level falls to 700 cost drivers, the actual cost will be $14.30, which is a significant difference in the cost.

A further issue is the nature of the cost drivers. These are usually "transactional" cost drivers where the number of times an activity has been carried out is important, such as the number of machine setups or the number of purchase orders raised. This assumes that the activities are homogeneous: All machine setups take the same time to carry out. Further analysis may show that there are differences in the *time* taken for setups, and we may improve our cost information if that is built into our model.

As ABC becomes more widely practiced, we can expect to see further modifications and refinements. This may also relate back to full costing and different methods of allocating overheads. However, the essence of the two approaches is shown in Table 2.5.

Table 2.5. Comparison of Full Costing and ABC

Full costing	ABC
Establish budget for overhead cost for the forthcoming financial period.	
Identify cost or profit centers over which total overheads will be shared.	Identify activity pools to which overheads will be collected.
Decide on allocation rate for each cost center. This will most likely be determined by machine hours, labor hours, or cost units.	Decide on the cost drivers for each activity pool. This is a factor that is capable of numerical measurement, such as the number of orders placed to purchase supplies.
Charge direct costs to the job, process, service, or activity.	
Charge indirect costs to products, jobs, or services using the allocation rate.	Charge indirect costs to the activity pool using the cost driver.
Add direct costs and indirect costs to find total cost or product, job, process, or activity.	

Time-Driven ABC

Kaplan and Anderson (2004)[6] recognized the weaknesses of ABC. One issue has been that the compilation of the time taken by various activities in an organization has been derived from interviews and surveys with individuals undertaking those activities. In a large organization, this can be very time-consuming and expensive. It is also an exercise that organizations would not wish to repeat frequently so the original estimates become outdated. One could also question the credibility of the data. There could be an understandable tendency for individuals to overestimate the time to demonstrate how hard they work!

The authors also questioned whether traditional ABC was suitable for complex operations. They pointed out that even shipping products could require a range of different approaches that could not be captured by a constant cost per order distributed.

Their proposed model simplifies ABC in two ways. First, managers are required to estimate on resources by each product, transaction, or customer. Two estimates are required: the cost per time unit of supplying resource capacity and the unit time of resource capacity consumption by each product, transaction, or customer. This provides the additional information on how many minutes that staff members spend on activities in a particular time period.

The authors have given guidance on how managers may best estimate these figures and then calculate the cost-driver rates. Time-driven ABC overcomes the difficulties and costs of implementing and maintaining a traditional ABC system and provides managers with cost and profit information quickly and inexpensively.

There have been several articles on variations of time-driven ABC and examples of organizations that have implanted it successfully. The proponents of the method write strongly in its favor, but we would not take this as encouragement for all organizations to adopt it. As we observed in chapter 1, it is for the organization to decide which system best meets its needs. In doing so, it will change and shape the system so that it fits the organization and not for the organization to fit the system.

Predetermined Overheads

In the previous discussions on both full and activity-based costing, we referred to the indirect costs without specifying the period of time in question. Upon reflection, you will realize that an organization cannot wait until the end of a financial period when the actual overhead amount is known. To do so would delay decision making and even the timely invoicing customers.

For this reason, overhead costs for the financial period, usually for a year, are predicted through a budgetary control system that we discuss in chapters 3 and 4. Using these predictions of the overhead costs, the allocation rate, whether machine hour or any other basis, is calculated and applied using the predicted figures.

Unfortunately, no matter how carefully budgets are determined, our financial predictions based on our strategy may not be completely valid. Also, we can expect that some of our predictions will not be 100% accurate. If that is the case, the overhead we are charging to the products and services we provide will be incorrect, and we will be in one of two situations.

In one situation, the amount of overhead we charge will be too high. This technically is known as overabsorption of overhead. The consequences can be dramatic. It is likely that the prices of products and services will be set too high, which will make the organization noncompetitive, and efforts will be made on cost reduction but will be misdirected.

In the other situation, the amount of overhead will be too low. Technically this is known as underabsorption, and the consequences are the reverse of the first situation. The organization may underprice its products and services and be operating at a loss.

To avoid the peril of these situations, the accountants keep a close eye on the overheads that were budgeted and those that are actually incurred. Adjustments can be made to correct the situation as the financial period progresses.

Job Costing for Manufacturing and Service Organizations

Identifying the Job

The type of work an organization chooses to undertake is the key component of its strategy. The purpose of job costing, also known as specific order costing, is to identify the cost of the job, whether it involves a tangible product or a particular service for a client.

You may have some preconceptions on what is a job. The following are examples:

- Your local garage servicing your car
- Workers building a bridge across a river
- A clinic conducting cosmetic surgery
- Guards providing security at an international meeting of politicians

A job has the following characteristics:

- It is an identifiable piece of work.
- It is carried out to a customer's specific requirements.
- Direct costs such as materials and labor can be identified with the job.

We will omit long-term jobs from our discussions, such as building a bridge, as these are also affected by financial accounting regulations and have their own characteristics. We will concern ourselves with work that is of short duration, normally under a year. In these circumstances each separate job is recognized as the cost object.

We have already explained the principles of full costing. This involves identifying the direct material and direct labor cost with the job. To this is added the share of the overheads. As each job is specific to the customer and the period of time the job takes is crucial, either the direct hours or machine hours taken for the job are used as the allocation rate.

One example of job costing you may be familiar with is taking your car to the garage for a service. Usually you receive an invoice that lists the parts fitted (direct materials) and also the time taken by the mechanic (direct labor). You will find that the rate charged for the mechanic's time is well above the actual pay rate. This is because it includes the allocation rate for the overhead. Garages usually use a labor hour rate to charge overheads to the job.

Calculating the Total Cost

Following is a worked example that illustrates all the stages in arriving at the full cost of a product. Once again, we simplified the calculations so you can concentrate on the principles used.

Danau Security Systems (DSS)

This is a small company that designs and installs security systems for commercial enterprises. It pays all the direct labor $10 per hour. The company uses full costing and has three production departments. With any job it does, the company adds 10% to the production cost of the job to cover the administration and selling of overheads and then adds a 5% mark-up to allow for profit. The data in Table 2.6 are available for the next financial year. These data will be used to share the factory overhead over the three departments using an arbitrary but reasonable basis.

Table 2.6. Data for Danau Security Systems

	Factory	Fabrication department	Assembly department	Installation department
Area (square meters)	2,000	1,000	600	400
Value of machinery ($)	100,000	60,000	30,000	10,000
Number of direct employed	80	20	40	20
Budgeted labor hours	15,000	3,500	7,500	4,000
Budgeted machine hours	13,800	12,000	1,800	—

Table 2.7. Overhead Analysis Statement

Overhead	Factory amount($)	Basis of allocation	Fabrication department ($)	Assembly department ($)	Installation department ($)
Rent	10,000	Area	5,000	3,000	2,000
Heat and light	16,000	Area	8,000	4,800	3,200
Building insurance	4,000	Area	2,000	1,200	800
Machinery insurance	15,000	Value of machinery	9,000	4,500	1,500
Supervisors' salaries	64,000	Number of employees	16,000	32,000	16,000
Contract cleaning	32,000	Number of employees	8,000	16,000	8,000
Totals	141,000		48,000	61,500	31,500

The company decides to use the machine hour rate in the fabrication department and the labor hour rate in the other two departments. According to Table 2.7, the machine hour rate in the fabrication department is $48,000 / 12,000 hours = $4.00 per hour. The labor hour rate in the assembly department is $61,500 / 7,500 hours = $8.20 and in the installation department, $31,500 / 4,000 hours = $7.875

Let us assume that a client, Global Sports, has agreed with DSS on the type of security system it requires and has asked for a quote for the job. DSS will draw up a job specification, and Table 2.8 shows a typical example. We have given you the amounts for the direct materials and labor so that the basis for charging the overheads can be clearly displayed. You should have little difficulty with the calculations if you remember our explanation in the first part of the chapter. This job passes through the three departments, and therefore the actual labor cost in each department must be charged at the rate of $10.00 per hour. In addition, a charge must be made for the overheads. In the fabrication department, machine hours are considered most important and the

Table 2.8. Global Sports Quote

Global Sports Job Specification

	$
Direct costs	
Direct materials	25,500
Direct labor	
Fabrication (620 hours)	6,200
Assembly (1,580 hours)	15,800
Installation (460 hours)	4,600
Total direct costs	52,100
Overhead allocation	
Fabrication (1,850 machine hours @ $4.00)	7,400
Assembly (1,580 labor hours @ $8.20)	12,956
Installation (460 labor hours @ $7.875)	3,623
Total production cost	**76,079**
Administration and selling overheads	7,607
	83,686
Profit markup	4,184
Selling price	87,870

overhead is calculated using the machine hour allocation rate. In the other two departments, labor hours are deemed to be most important, but remember that the labor hour allocation rate for overheads must be used, *not* the pay rate.

There are two important points that need to be made on the managerial aspect of the statement as follows:

- It is both a plan and a control document. If Danau Security Systems wins this job, it will use the job specification to control the progress of the job.
- The figures are predictions, but there is little scope for error. If the overheads are incorrectly predetermined, the profit could quickly turn into a loss.

Danau could have used a "blanket" rate for factory overheads instead of the departmental rate. This would mean that the total overheads of $141,000 would be divided by the total predicted labor hours of 15,000 to give an overhead recovery rate of $9.40. If you multiply this rate by the total labor hours the result is an overhead charge of 2,660 × $9.40. This gives an overhead charge for the job of $25,004 compared to the amount on the job specification of $23,979.

Which one is right? The answer is that both are "right" within the logic of the method you are using, but you will find that a departmental rate is likely to give you more precise information for control and decision making than a blanket rate.

This returns us to the theme raised in chapter 1, which is the cost of costing. Strategic cost information can be extremely detailed and precise. But to contribute to the organization it must be available by the time required and should not be more expensive to generate than the perceived value it contributes. In chapter 6, we examine more comprehensive strategic cost techniques. With each of these, the question needs to be asked whether it is a value-added activity.

In some industries it is sometimes possible to negotiate the price of a job on a cost plus policy. The final selling price is calculated by adding an agreed fixed-profit margin to the cost of the job. This approach has a number of weaknesses, as there is no incentive to control the cost of the job. It ignores market conditions, and the total costs are dependent on the method of overhead recovery. If a client does enter into such a contract, it is essential that the job specification is agreed in minute detail.

As a final note on specific order operations, remember the nature of the activity being undertaken. In some industries, certain jobs are so repetitive and financially minor that the company does not need to cost each job. Everyday examples are oil changes for your car, visits to the dental hygienist, or printing business cards. Although there is a customer (yourself) and the job is specifically for you, the service provider usually has a standard price based on previous experience. This "average" cost is deemed sufficiently precise to determine strategy.

Costing in the Services Sector

Defining the Service Sector

Frequently text books will refer to "service costing" as if it is a separate method used from those that we have discussed in this chapter. In our opinion, there is no specific method of costing devised just for service activities. To support this, we give the following quote from Rezzae:

> Banks, like manufacturing firms, use either standard or actual cost systems. The two basic costing methods used by banks are unit costs and cost allocations. Ironically, these are the tools of any cost accounting system and the basics are not unique to banking.[7]

However, there are certain attributes of service operations that emphasize specific features of the basic costing method applied. Even a brief examination will identify the following features.

- The organizations are frequently national or international operations with a complicated management structure.
- A range of services may be offered, sometimes very different in nature.
- Products may be manufactured in addition to the services provision.

At a more detailed level, Modell[8] extracted from the relevant literature the following characteristics that differ in service organizations from manufacturing.

- As service organizations usually have little inventory, the distinction between product and period costs are not relevant.
- It is difficult to separate service organization's costs into their fixed and variable elements.
- Specific costs are not easily traceable to certain revenue or output items.
- A substantial share of the costs are overheads.

As for the last point, it has been estimated that between 60% and 85% of total costs in U.S. health care institutions are classified as fixed, with a substantial proportion of that being labor costs.[9]

Determining the Cost Object

Some of the aspects of service operations that should be taken into account when identifying the cost object are

- the insignificance of cost of materials,
- the significance of direct labor.

Allocation of overheads is far more complicated than in a manufacturing organization.

It may be difficult to define the cost object, and hypothetical ones must be generated. For example, a hotel may decide on an occupied bed night or a transport company on a hybrid measure combining weight and distance mile.

Because of these features, some trends have emerged in recent years, and articles have been published that give a guide to practices in the service sector. If we consider the two methods to identify the total cost of an activity, both full costing and activity-based costing are used. In service organizations where a sensible cost object can be devised or where there are identifiable jobs, the procedures we have explained in this chapter can be applied for the allocation of overheads and the calculation of an allocation rate. But given the differing characteristics of service organizations, it is not surprising that new costing techniques, such as activity-based costing (ABC), aimed at allocating costs to various activities are attracting significant interest and application

Process Costing in Manufacturing

The Issues

Key Definition

Process costing is used where there are continuous operations in manufacturing, and a stream of homogeneous products flow from one process to the next until the production is complete.

The costing method is used where the production process is carried out in a series of separate stages with identifiable inputs and outputs at each stage. The finished output at one stage of production becomes the input for the next stage. Each stage or process can usually be clearly identified and is often contained in a separate department.

At each separate stage, both direct and indirect costs are calculated. Direct costs for a particular process can be identified from the accounting records. Overheads will be allocated to the separate processes in the way we described under full costing. The average cost of each cost object can be calculated at each stage by simply dividing the total cost of that process for a period of time by the number of cost objects produced in that period. The costs for the cost objects are aggregated to give the final total cost for all the processes that production goes through.

If you refer back to our discussion on overhead allocation, you will see that we are using the basis of dividing total costs for a period of time by the number of cost objects produced. Alternative methods such as machine hours or labor hours would not be relevant.

Simple as this method of costing is, there is an additional problem that occurs at the end of each financial period. We know the number of units completed during the financial period and transferred as inputs to the next process. A number of cost objects are not completed by the end of the financial period for each of the separate processes. We need to know the cost of these incomplete units.

You will find that some accounting textbooks devote considerable space in demonstrating the calculations in detail. This is essentially to provide the required information for financial accounts, and the usefulness of these calculations for the *management* of processes is doubtful.

In our explanation of process costing, we therefore use a simplified approach that demonstrates fully the principles without becoming entangled in the detail. In the following example, we are assuming that a company has two separate processes in the production flow. The completed outputs from Process 1 are transferred to Process 2 as the inputs for that process. For each process, the direct materials, direct labor, and a share of the overheads for that financial period are identified.

If there was not the problem of incomplete units at the end of the financial period, the calculations are easy. Assume that in the month of January a company that has two processes has the following information for Process 1:

Direct materials ($)	12,000
Direct labor ($)	3,000
Overheads ($)	5,000
Total production cost ($)	20,000

The number of completed units transferred to Process 2 during the period was 80,000.

There were no incomplete units in Process 1 at the end of the period.

average cost per completed unit for the period $20,000 / 80,000 = $0.25

Equivalent Units

Let us now introduce the problem of incomplete units and the concept of "equivalent units." If a unit is not complete at the end of the financial period, it will not be transferred to Process 2 but will remain in Process 1 to be completed. This will incur additional costs in the next financial period to complete the units. What we need to know is how much it has cost us in January in Process 1 to produce these incomplete units: the work in process (WIP).

The answer to finding their cost is to use the concept of equivalent units. If at the end of January there were 5,000 units that had been only 50% completed, we would say that these were the equivalent of 2,500 completed units. We have calculated that the cost of a completed unit is $0.25, so the cost of our 5,000 incomplete units is 2,500 × $0.25 = $625.

You most likely have several comments on this calculation. The first will be on the somewhat imprecise nature of the calculation. We could, with time and effort, obtain a more accurate figure, but it is highly doubtful that information would improve your control of operations and your decision making.

Your second comment may be on the assumption that 50% completion of the unit means that 50% of the cost has been incurred. We address that issue in the next example, where we look at Process 2 for the same company for the month of February.

Resolving the Issues

The information we use to construct Table 2.9 is as follows:

- The 80,000 completed cost objects have been transferred from Process 1 at the end of January.
- At the end of February, there are 78,000 units completed, and there are 2,000 units incomplete that form work in process.
- With the 2,000 units that form work in process, obviously all the costs are complete for Process 1, otherwise the units would not have been transferred.
- Direct material cost for Process 2 has been completed.
- The cost objects are 50% complete as far as direct labor and overheads are concerned.

Explanatory Notes

1. Previous process costs are always complete if products are transferred to the next process. Incomplete units will not be transferred to the next process.
2. The average cost per unit in column 6 is calculated by dividing the total cost per item (column 2) by the number of effective units (column 5).
3. Process 2 has 78,000 completed units at the end of the financial period. Of the remaining 2,000, the costs are complete from Process

Table 2.9. Process 2: Costs for February

1	2	3	4	5	6	7
Nature of cost	Total cost ($)	Number of completed units	Equivalent units in WIP	Effective units	Average cost per unit ($)	Value of WIP ($)
From process 1	20,000	78,000	2,000	80,000	0.25	500
Direct materials	30,000	78,000	2,000	80,000	0.375	750
Direct labor	11,850	78,000	1,000	79,000	0.15	150
Overheads	23,700	78,000	1,000	79,000	0.30	300
Total	85,550				1.075	1,700
Reconciliation and Summary						
Value of completed units (78,000 × $1.075)	$83,850					
Value of WIP (column 7)	$1,700					
Total cost (reconciles with column 1)	$85,550					

1 and for materials but only 50% complete for direct labor and over-heads. This gives us the value of WIP.

4. Abnormal losses or gains should not be included in the costs of the products.

5. Where the output from one process is developed into two or more different products, the technique of joint process costing will be applied.

The method of costing for processes is fairly straightforward, and the attention given to it in some textbooks is misapplied. It is not as important for strategic costing as you may think. It is important for financial accounting where it is essential to identify the full cost of the products and the value of inventory. In support of this contention, we refer to a study of three companies that discovered the process costing practices were different from that described in management texts. In fact, the companies paid considerable effort on developing accurate standard input costs and volumes rather than the information from process costing to help manage business operations efficiently and effectively.[10] We explain standard costing in the following chapter.

Process costing is useful to record the costs of the manufacturing activity, but it is essential to view it in the context of other methods and techniques companies use as part of their strategic costing management.

Conclusions

This chapter has considered different approaches to calculate what a product or service costs. The first step is to determine the classification of costs. The main types discussed in this chapter are direct costs and indirect costs. Charging direct costs to what is being costed is merely a matter of having good procedures and record keeping. The indirect costs or overheads cause a problem, and the two different solutions are full (absorption costing) and activity-based costing, whether traditional or time-driven.

Full costing, as demonstrated in our explanations of job costing and process costing, has two features:

- The predetermined overheads of the financial period are shared over the production departments in a fair but arbitrary manner.

- The overheads for that production department are charged to the units passing through it using mainly number of cost units, machine hours, or labor hours.

Activity-based costing has emerged as an alternative to absorption costing because of changes in manufacturing operations and the growth of the service sector. The greater application of technology, the use of techniques such as JIT, and the reduction and change in the nature of direct labor have meant that traditional costing methods are not providing sufficiently accurate information for decision-making purposes.

ABC is a costing system in which costs are first assigned to pools, and then cost drivers are used to calculate the total cost of specified activities. ABC offers the advantage of more accurate information than absorption costing because it looks for a closer relationship between overheads and the cause of these indirect costs. However, it suffers from the disadvantage that it is costly to implement and operate. The procedure for ABC is to identify the following:

- Cost pools, which are identifiable activity centers that perform an operation that uses resources
- Cost drivers that cause a change in the activities of the cost pool
- Cost driver rates by dividing the costs of the cost pool by the units of activities

Because of the difficulties and cost of implementing traditional ABC, a simplified method known as time-driven ABC has been devised, and advocates claim it offers several advantages.

We argued in this chapter that there are no specific costing methods for service organizations, but there are certain features that need to be addressed:

- The organizations are frequently national or international operations with a complicated management structure.
- A range of services may be offered, sometimes very different in nature.

- Products may be manufactured in addition to the services provision.
- It is sometimes difficult to identify the cost object.

The evidence available suggests that activity-based costing is most useful in service organizations where complexity of operations and the cost object are not assessed successfully by full costing. As with all costing methods and techniques, you need to ask whether it provides the cost information you require to construct and successfully achieve the corporate strategy.

CHAPTER 3

Establishing Plans

About This Chapter

Planning is the part of strategic cost analysis that is crucial to decisions on corporate strategy. Your ability to plan and control the costs of activities for which you have responsibility is essential to ensuring that organizational strategy is viable and capable of being pursued successfully. In this chapter, we explain the planning process and your probable involvement. In the next chapter, you will learn how to use the financial information generated from the techniques we discuss here to monitor and control your own responsibilities.

Strategic cost planning will involve the consideration of various scenarios and determining which plans will attain the desired objectives. To achieve both short-term and long-term goals, progress toward them must be monitored and controlled by managers regularly comparing and analyzing actual performance against the plans.

In your organization, you will find that one or both of two techniques explained in this chapter are used. Standard costing concentrates on the daily operations and the continued achievement of short-term goals. Although a method routinely used in large manufacturing organizations, it can also be used in the service sector. The technique is very close to the daily production process and the relationship between inputs and outputs.

Budgetary control is concerned with the proposed strategy over a longer time period. The long-term strategy is determined, usually for one year, and periodic monthly subgoals set toward the proposed strategy. Budgetary control, in various forms of sophistication, is found in nearly all types and sizes of organizations. It would be unusual for a manager not to be monitoring and controlling the activities for which they are responsible without a budget. It is also the one topic where the application of performance measures and human behavior are most frequently observed.

In this chapter, we first explain standard costing and discuss the different aspects of setting the standards and where you may be involved. Because of the importance of budgetary control in most organizations, the concepts and principles of the subject will be a major part of this chapter.

Standard Costing

Setting Standards

Key Definition

Standard costing is a system of cost ascertainment and control in which predetermined standard costs and income from products and operations are set and periodically compared with actual costs incurred and income generated in order to establish any variances.[1]

It is important to bear in mind that in conducting an analysis, the total cost of a resource is a result of two factors: the usage or quantity of that resource and the price per unit of that resource. If we are going to conduct an analysis that captures the interaction of these two variables, we need a technique that does the same. Standard costing allows us to conduct a detailed analysis of the factors.

In the previous chapter, we noted that process costing, in many organizations, is accompanied by standard costing to ensure that managerial monitoring and control of costs is achieved. Standard costing therefore sets out certain levels of performance and measures actual performance against that standard. Any difference, known as a variance, is investigated.

Standards can be set for various activities, but in this section we will use material and labor costs as exemplars, as they illustrate the technique and are the standards most commonly found. You may not be involved with material and labor costs, but the principles we demonstrate are transferable to other areas of activity. In the next chapter, you will learn how to analyze the information arising from the standard costs of other activities.

Note that in the aforementioned definition, reference is made both to costs incurred and to income generated. Standard costing is used to examine differences between the planned revenue and actual revenue and not only to investigate costs. In our discussions, we explain how standard costing can be applied to revenue.

To establish standards of performance for an organization, the working conditions must be defined and a decision made as to whether ideal or attainable standards should be set. Ideal standards are based on the best possible working conditions and usually assume that operations are at full capacity with no wastage, breakdowns, or idle time. Although ideal standards present a rigorous approach, the fact that they are unlikely to be achievable can demotivate employees and distort the strategic plans. Attainable standards are more widely used because they are based on realistic efficient performance and allow for potential, but acceptable, deviations from perfect performance.

The philosophy and strategic and financial sophistication of an organization will determine the approach to its standard setting. Some of these approaches do not have any analytical basis and are little more than repeating past mistakes, as you can conclude from the following list.

- A prior period's level of performance. Although this may reflect the successes of the past, it may also include the deficiencies and not take into account changes in both internal and external conditions that may have taken place.
- The levels achieved by comparable organizations. This is a more analytical approach and has certain competitive attractions, but caution must be used to ensure true comparability.
- A backward-looking assessment of what should have been achieved. This "after the event" approach rarely provides credible data for monitoring and control.
- The levels of performance that the company wishes to achieve in order to pursue its strategic plans.

You need to understand the basis used by your organization to set standards, as this represents the performance levels you are expected to achieve. You may find that your organization involves you fully in setting the standards for your area of responsibility or asks you to comment on the feasibility of the standards set.

To integrate usage and price, the standard cost is the planned unit of cost that is calculated from technical specifications and economic and market conditions. The technical specifications specify the quantity of materials, labor, and other elements of cost required, and these are then related to the prices and wages that are expected to be in place during the period when the standard cost will be used.

To determine the appropriate standard for both usage and price of a resource, a careful analysis must be conducted on a range of information. To set standards for materials and labor, the organization will refer to the following:

- **Materials: quantity and price**
  - Analysis of past data
  - Job specifications, which should list required materials
  - Engineering plans that provide a list of materials
  - Chemical formulas
  - Recipes or other documents specifying materials required
  - Time and motion studies
  - Price lists provided by suppliers
  - Expected economic environment
  - Predicted actions of suppliers, competitors, and customers
- **Labor: quantity (hours) and rate**
  - Analysis of past data
  - Time and motion studies
  - Contracts that set labor rates
  - Prevailing rates in the area or industry
  - Expected economic environment
  - Changes in labor supply and demand

As a procurement manager you can expect to be involved in the materials pricing standard. As an engineer, chemist, or production manager you will assist with the quantity of the materials. Similarly with labor standards, a range of managerial knowledge and experience may be called in to assist in setting standards.

At this stage, you will realize that standards are going to be set for the cost of the inputs, the labor, and the materials, and you therefore need to know the price for the inputs and the amount of usage for a certain level of production. The total cost of a particular input will be the amount used multiplied by the price paid for a specific quantity of that output.

Applying this principle, the use of 30 meters of a particular material at $2.00 per meter will have a total cost of $60.00.

One difference in setting standards is that for labor. With this input, we are interested in the planned time that direct labor will take to complete a certain volume of work. This is usually measured in standard hours or standard minutes. The important point is that a standard hour is a measure of production output, rather than a measure of actual time. For example, a company may determine that 600 cost units should be produced in 1 hour. In a 7-hour day, the actual total production is 4,800 cost units. That actual output can be converted into standard hours as follows:

4,800 units / 600 = 8 standard hours of production.

You will appreciate that if you have managed to achieve 8 standard hours of production in 7 actual hours, labor is being very efficient. In the next section, we will examine how this achievement can be measured in financial terms and integrated into a cohesive analysis of the activities.

Calculating the Variances

A variance is the difference between the standard or planned level of performance and the actual performance achieved. In this case, we are interested in analyzing the cost performance. To do this successfully, we need to know the interaction between the usage and price of a resource to give the total cost.

A simple example will demonstrate the calculation of the standard and the variance. Suppose that you intend to make some fruit juice, and you decide to buy oranges. Your investigations establish that you require 50 pounds of oranges for the quantity of juice you want. A survey of fruit suppliers shows that the price would be $1.20 per pound. The total cost to you would therefore be

50 pounds × $1.20 = $60,

and this is your standard. Unfortunately, when you buy the oranges, you find they are of an inferior quality. Now, you need 60 pounds, but the price is only $1.10 per pound, giving a total cost of $66.

Say that you compare your total material cost to your standard, and you have an adverse or unfavorable variance of $6.00 because you paid more in total than you planned. This can be expressed using the following formula:

(standard quantity × standard price) − (actual quantity × actual price)

(50 pounds × $1.20) − (60 pounds ×$1.10) = $6.00 unfavorable (U).

At this stage, we have information on the total cost, but we need to pursue our analysis further. We need to know the financial consequences of buying more oranges than you planned (a quantity variance) and that of paying less per pound than you planned (a price variance). The following formulas can be used:

quantity variance: (SQ − AQ) × SP = (50 − 60) × $1.20 = $12.00 U

price variance: (SP − AP) × AQ = ($1.20 − $1.10) × 60 = $6.00 F.

The two subvariances of quantity and price can be netted off to give the total variance. In this example, we have referred to a quantity variance. In some organizations, they will calculate the amount of materials purchased, not necessarily used, and in others they will calculate the actual usage and refer to it as the usage variance.

The more detailed analysis informs us on the interaction between the usage and price of the resource on the total cost. From this, we can make decisions on the quality of materials we are using and the price we have to pay for each unit of the material.

In the next chapter, you will learn how to calculate and analyze variances: the differences between the standards set and the actual performance achieved. It is this information that contributes to strategic cost analysis. At this stage of setting the standards, you will appreciate that there are many organizational benefits to be gained:

- The practice of using past performance as a guide is removed, and the standards demonstrate the strategic plans of the organization.
- Standards are set for future activities, and they encourage managers in making decisions aligned to strategic priorities.

- Implementing standards requires a thorough examination of the organization's production and operations activities. Every stage in production is minutely examined, and the most cost-effective and efficient procedures are established.
- Responsibility for performance is identified with specific managers.
- A viable and credible benchmark is established, against which actual performance can be compared.
- The setting of standards encourages the coordination and integration of the various functional activities.
- The regular updating of standards encourages a continuous review of activities.
- Where managers are properly trained (as they should be) in the investigation and analysis of standards, they will become more effective.

Although standard costing offers many organizational benefits, there are aspects that you need to consider when assessing the implementation and maintenance of the system:

- In a turbulent economic environment or where the organization is breaking new frontiers, it may be impossible to gather sufficiently robust data to set viable standards.
- Even with a fairly simple system, implementing and updating a system can be costly.
- If any of the standards become out of date or lose their relevance, the entire system has reduced credibility.
- Busy managers may suffer from information overload and ignore the data.

One of the considerable advantages of standard costing is its flexibility in application. You need not have a full-blown system covering all aspects of the organization. You may only set standards for material usage if that is a significant cost and you wish to ensure tight control. In the following chapter, we cover a wide range of different standards. It is important that you are selective in the standards that are of benefit to you. Also remember that there are other control methods that may be more appropriate in certain conditions.

Budgetary Control: Overview

The importance of budgets to strategy formulation cannot be overemphasized. A recent study found that in most organizations the budget process is explicitly linked to strategy implementation. Indeed, budgeting was identified as an important means for implementing strategy.[2] As a manager, in probability, you will be involved in establishing the budget for your area of responsibility.

A budget is a financial representation of the strategy of an organization. In constructing a budget, a careful analysis of all planned costs needs to be conducted and the choice of alternative courses of action assessed.

A typical budget

- relates to a defined time period (usually 12 months divided into shorter periods),
- is designed and approved well in advance of the period to which it relates,
- shows expected income and expenditure,
- identifies responsibility levels for various parts of the budget,
- includes all capital and revenue expenses likely to be incurred in furthering the organization's strategic objectives,
- is not an accounting exercise but a managerial planning and control system.

Functional budgets will be constructed based on departments or some other identifiable area of activity. These functional budgets will be integrated to form the master budget that encompasses all the organization's operations and activities.

To ensure monitoring and control of actual performance against the budget, an analysis of differences arising between the actual and planned performance needs to be conducted regularly. Managers responsible for governing costs allocated to their centers should investigate any differences. You will learn in the next chapter how to assess and investigate these variances.

We emphasize that a budget should be released well in advance of the financial period. It is usual that this will not occur until the board or governing body of the organization has given its approval. Because of the substantial amount of work required in generating, integrating, and obtaining approval of the budget, they are sometimes issued after the financial period has commenced. Unfortunately, all too commonly managers spend the first few months of a new financial period working to an informal budget or even using last year's budget as a benchmark.

If your organization is not efficient and issues budgets after the start of the operating period, you are at a disadvantage. Without the details of the organizational strategy that are encompassed in the budget, you have no platform to manage successfully. If you are working in such an organization, make it very clear to your superiors what basis you are using as a plan. It may be the budget for last year or the actual performance for last year. Do not fall into the trap of agreeing to manage as best as you can.

Advantages of Budgetary Control

You now have the broad picture of what budgetary control is about, but you may wonder whether all the work involved is of benefit. We return to that issue at the end of the chapter, but we first consider the advantages of budgetary control:

- Strategic formulation and implementation is enabled by the formal planning process.
- Control and assessment of actual performance is ensured by the regular and frequent comparisons with planned performance.
- Corrective action can be taken in a timely manner where actual performance is unacceptable, or unforeseen economic events intrude.
- Coordination of the various organizational functions is established.
- Communication to all managers of organizational objectives and progress toward them is achieved.

- Responsibility of managers for the performance of activities and functions within their control is clearly determined and reported upon.
- Consensus on organizational objectives and motivation to achieve them is developed through a carefully conducted budgetary control process.
- A comprehensive analysis is conducted of all costs incurred by the organization.

Approaches to Budgetary Control

Most advice is that budgetary control is improved in an organization where the process is participative; managers are involved in establishing the budgets for their own particular function or level of responsibility. In practice, it is frequently less clear how this is to be achieved and the benefits of coordination of activities enjoyed within a reasonable time period.

Setting budgets takes a significant amount of your managerial time, and the greater the amount of discussion and participation, the longer the process is likely to take. One of the requirements of a good system of budgetary control is that the budgets are prepared, agreed, and disseminated *prior* to the commencement of the financial period.

This will mean that you are trying to make plans for a future period. If the budget period starts in January 2013, you may be asked in October 2012 to contribute to setting the plans for your own area for the forthcoming year. In other words, in October 2012, you will be attempting to determine your activities for the months of October, November, and December 2013, as well as the preceding months. This is a test of your managerial skills and the issues you should assess are the possible

- changes in the size of the organization's market and its market share;
- competitors' strategies;
- changes in interest rates or exchange rates;
- sources and costs of external funding;
- changes in costs and availability of energy, materials, and labor;
- changes in legislation, social pressures, environmental concerns that will affect the organization;

- effects of the activities of other related organizations;
- changes in climate, consumer demographics, or foreign political powers;
- actions and influences of global bodies.

You will appreciate that setting budgets is not merely about predicting the future. By setting out the organizational *financial and managerial strategies* and the actions that must be taken to achieve them, managers at all levels are making business plans that help meet the financial objectives.

The approach to budgeting will depend on a number of factors from the prevailing style of management to the funding of the organization. We discuss three approaches found in practice. You should bear in mind that in some organizations, all three approaches may be operating simultaneously in different parts of the company.

Top-Down Budgets

With this approach, budgets are determined at the most senior level in the organization and there is little or no participation by managers. You will find that most textbooks decry this approach to budgeting, but there are specific reasons why you find this in practice. Because academics may find that it does not correspond with their managerial philosophy, does not mean that the system is of no value to the organization. We have identified the following reasons for the top-down approach.

Managerial Style

There are senior managers who believe that it is their responsibility to manage and that authority is held at the top positions in the organization. In a particularly turbulent economic environment, decisions may need to be made quickly, and participative budgeting may enhance the decision making process, but it will undoubtedly slow it down.

Sources of Funding

Many organizations do not have control of the generation of their own revenue. If you consider government organizations, they rely on tax dollars for their funding. Usually, departments and various bodies will carry out political lobbying to obtain their share of the tax revenue. The decision on the allocation is made at the top and will often be passed down together with a list of priorities that must be achieved. The opportunity for managers to participate in the allocation is constrained by the political decisions.

Similarly, organizations such as charities and art, community, sport, and other groups will be heavily reliant on donations and bequests. Although considerable effort may be made to improve the inflow of dollars, to a large extent budget strategy will concentrate on spending the dollars effectively under the mandate they have.

The Markets

It is easy to forget that directors are not making decisions in a vacuum. They are answerable to their shareholders and, possibly more dauntingly, the analysts and the stock markets. Also, the performance of the organization, as measured by earnings and various ratios, will be compared to its competitors. The market will have certain expectations, and the board must shape its strategic plans to meet, and if possible beat, these expectations.

Company Size

There is evidence from the United Kingdom that in businesses of 10–15 employees, the owner-managers impose budgets, if there are any, that must be rigidly adhered to by junior managers.[3] One would anticipate that, in many small businesses, budgetary control is basic, and the full concentration may be on the cash inflows and outflows, and owners may consider that private information.

Although we can identify reasons for top-down budgeting, it does have its problems. Frequently, managerial initiative is heavily constrained by the requirement to comply with the budget. You may find yourself becoming demotivated and not search for savings or ways to improve the performance of the company. If you understand the principles and procedures of budgetary control, as explained in this book, you can make a valuable contribution to your company's success, which is usually recognized.

Bottom-Up Budgets

With this approach, budgets are gradually built up from input from the managers most closely connected with particular activities and functions. The arguments in favor of this approach are strong but not totally persuasive. The philosophy is that full participation by those most closely affected by the budgetary control system will lead to more realistic plans, employees will be more highly motivated and organizational performance will be improved.

There are examples where organizations have encouraged a high degree of employee participation in the budgetary control system and have apparently enjoyed improved performance. Of course, these examples are often of companies that are well organized and financially secure. It can be difficult to prove that participation in budgets was the sole reason for success. Sometimes, where a company has been in financial distress, working cooperatively with employees has turned the company around. Closer examination will usually show that the success may be more likely due to agreed wage cuts, and thus reduced labor costs, and efficiency and productivity improvements that needed to be introduced in any event.

Scenario Planning

In various forms, organizations have found that this approach permits participation, enhances integration, maintains a strategic approach, and can be accomplished within a reasonable time frame. The first stage is for senior managers to obtain forecasts, often from external agencies, of various economic indicators, such as exchange rates, inflation, market growth or decline, material availability, or consumer confidence.

For the next stage, an organization may select one scenario or alternative scenarios and the strategies that could be pursued. This information is then distributed to managers for their inputs. Depending on the company's policy, the managers may be able to select the scenario or strategy they find most credible. Having made this selection, the manager then establishes the budget for his or her section.

The less choice of scenarios and strategies that the manager can select from, the quicker the process and the easier to attempt to integrate the various management inputs into one cohesive master budget.

Developing Budgets

Incremental Budgeting

With this type of budgeting system, the new budget is set by adding or deducting an incremental percentage to either the current year's actual income and expenditure or the present budget. This can be as unsophisticated as merely adding a percentage to all items to allow for inflation. At a more sophisticated level, there may be varying amounts of incremental increase to recognize some required or desired changes in activities. The organization usually has assumed that it is in a stable environment where planned performance is relatively certain and consistent from one year to the next. This type of budget has the following advantages and disadvantages.

- **Advantages**
  - The system is simple and quick to implement.
  - Managers are not confronted by significant changes in operations and the consequent demands on their time.
  - The integration of functional budgets is maintained and interdepartmental relationships kept consistent.
  - If activities become suddenly constrained by external forces, the organization may have no choice but to cut all budgets and is therefore recognizing the reality of these constraints and can do so quickly.
- **Disadvantages**
  - The deficiencies in actual performance or previous budgets are repeated.
  - The assumption is that the organization is successful and will remain so. Consequently, little or no strategic planning takes place.
  - There is no motivation for managers to look for cost reduction or efficiency gains.
  - There is no effort to achieve improved performance levels.
  - There is the tendency for managers to spend their budgets to ensure they will receive an equivalent amount in the next budget.

Zero-Base Budgeting

This approach was pioneered in commercial organizations by Texas Instruments as "Objectives, Strategies and Tactics." The concept was developed by Peter A. Pyhrr, and in a *Harvard Review* article he called it zero-base budgeting.[4] The essence of the concept, which has changed little over the years, is that the onus is placed firmly on each manager to develop his or her budget from scratch. In other words, the costs of all activities must be justified by you as a manager from a zero base, unlike incremental budgeting where current actual performance or budget is a benchmark to which agreed increments are added or deducted.

This approach means that no operations, activities, or expenses are automatically funded merely because they already exist. This makes the budget much more relevant to the particular conditions expected in the budget period and the strategy to be pursued rather than incremental budgeting. It places a substantial demand on you as a manager to prove the valuable and essential contribution your area of responsibility makes to the organization's success.

Organizations using zero-base budgeting will develop their own individual approach, but there are usually three main stages.

- *Stage 1.* The organizational objectives and strategies are spelled out in as much detail as possible. The question being asked is "What are we trying to do and how will we do it in the environment we anticipate?" You will note that the predicted environment is essential to the question. The various levels where managers will be responsible for determining the budget are identified.
- *Stage 2.* Managers at these levels must spell out the specific activities they will conduct to meet the organization's strategy and the budget required. Wherever possible, alternative methods should be proposed with their costs and advantages and disadvantages. You should also incorporate your opinion on the implications of not conducting that activity.
- *Stage 3.* The activities and how they will be conducted at each decision level are then selected. This is usually conducted by top management to ensure the efficient integration of all the

functions. You would not want the distribution department to be closed if another manager's budget was based on the assumption that it would remain in operation!

As can be envisaged, this procedure is expensive and time consuming but does have analytical rigor. Most organizations will only implement zero-base budgeting where there are significant changes anticipated or new ventures are to be undertaken. Some organizations find it useful to conduct partial zero-base budgeting in different parts of the organization at various times. You may find it useful to carry out an informal zero-base approach on your own responsibility area. It may provide useful illumination on how to improve your performance.

Rolling Budgets

Both incremental budgets and zero-base budgets suffer from the same problem. They are set prior to the commencement of the financial year, and given the speed of change and general uncertainty in the external environment, they can become soon outdated. Assuming that much of the decision making that goes into them gets done in the fourth quarter of the prior year, by the end of the following year, traditional budgets reflect thinking and data more than 12 months old. One response to this is the use of rolling budgets.

These can take many forms but the main concept is that prior or present actual performance is used as a basis for setting budgets for near future performance. For example, a company may be monitoring monthly performance. It will use actual performance over the last 12 months as the basis for establishing the budget for the next 3 months. As each month passes, the company extends its time frame into the future using recent actual performance as a guide.

Activity-Based Budgeting

Activity-based costing was examined in chapter 2, and it is a logical step to move the concepts into the budgeting process. It is essentially a reversal of an ABC system. In ABC, the movement is from the resources to the activities and then finally to the products and customers. In ABB, the movement is from forecast of the products and customers to the activities to achieve this forecast and finally to the resources required to support the activities. The main difference with ABB from traditional budgeting is found in the treatment of overheads. Traditional budgeting calculates the cost of operating an organizational unit, such as a department. ABB constructs a budget based on the demands of a particular activity for resources.

A simple example using a flexed budget illustrates the principles. Compare this to earlier examples in this chapter where the concentration was on a department and the production output. Now we are concentrating on the cost driver of machine hours.

A production department has a separate maintenance function and has determined that its cost driver is machine hours, which is an ABC measure. For two financial periods, the fixed cost of the maintenance department is $30,000, and the variable cost per machine hour is $3.00. In the first financial period, it is predicted there will be 6,000 machine hours and in the second period 7,000 machine hours. The budget for the two periods is shown in Table 3.1. By using machine hours and a flexible budget, we have been able to capture the different demands on resources and the impact of variations on activity.

The claimed advantages of ABB mirror the claimed advantages of activity-based costing. You should be better able to identify the resources you require, and this will lead to realistic budgets that are closely related to strategy. It also links the resource costs to the expected outputs and defines your responsibilities as a manager over certain activities.

Take a few words of caution: Do not be surprised if your organization does not exactly follow the models you find in textbooks. As stated in chapter 1, organizational systems are a function of environmental and firm-specific factors. They are also there to help develop and achieve the strategic objectives of the organization.

Table 3.1. Budget for Two Financial Periods

			First period	Second period
	Fixed cost	Variable cost	6,000 machine hours	7,000 machine hours
Maintenance function	$30,000	$3.00	$48,000	$51,000

Budget Implementation

Basic Requirements

The ability to conduct strategic cost analysis will depend on the effectiveness of the budget system. There are several criteria that should be satisfied for an effective budgetary control system. Indeed the list can be so long as to deter any organization from adopting budgetary control. We list below what can be considered to be the main features, and you should check to ascertain whether these are present in your own place of work.

- Organizational
  - A sound and clearly defined organization
  - Effective accounting records and procedures that are understood and applied
  - The recognition at all levels that budgetary control is a strategic activity and not an accounting exercise
  - Strong support and the commitment of top managers to the system of budgetary control
- Managerial
  - Managers responsibilities for areas of activity are clearly identified
  - The education and training of managers in the development, interpretation, and use of budgets
  - The participation of managers in the budgetary control system
- Procedural
  - Budget decisions are made in a timely manner before the commencement of a financial period
  - An information system that provides data for managers so they can make realistic predictions
  - The correct integration of budgets and their effective communication to managers
  - Regular feedback on actual performance against budget so that corrective action can be taken

Budget Centers

Organizations usually draw up individual budgets for each budget center. There are typically departments, functions of the business, or any other activity where a manager will be responsible for the monitoring and control of that budget center. As a manager you can expect to receive a budget and to be responsible for ensuring that you meet the budget and can explain any divergences.

A budget center can, financially, have different forms that will affect the manager's responsibilities and the issues that have to be addressed. Table 3.2 shows the type of budget center, the manager's responsibility, and the problems.

Budgetary control is frequently referred to as responsibility accounting, and Table 3.2 shows why. By regular financial performance reports, early feedback is provided to the manager for corrective action, performance assessment, and evaluation of strategy.

In Table 3.2, we have referred to the controllability of costs by the budget center manager. The concept and reality of controllability is hard to define, as a manager is rarely the only person in the organization that can influence certain costs. Also, some costs may be controllable in the short term but not the long term. Uncontrollable costs can usually be identified as the responsibility of senior management and often include the allocation of overheads.

Table 3.2. Budget Center Responsibilities and Problems

Type of center	Manager's responsibility	Issues
Cost	To manage costs within the limits of the budget	Some costs will be controllable and the manager can influence them. Some costs may be uncontrollable by the manager.
Revenue	To generate revenue to the level of or above that in the budget	Frequently found in financial institutions and retailers, managers have no control over costs but must meet or exceed the sales budget with their allocated resources.
Profit	To control revenue and costs to meet the profit in the budget	Profit can be calculated in many ways and the manager needs to understand the definitions of costs and revenues in the budget.
Investment	To manage the center as if it is an independent entity	This is a large portfolio, and the degree of autonomy in decision making needs to be agreed.

As a manager, you will use the budget to work toward the strategic goals of the organization. The budgetary system therefore needs to be clear, transparent, and credible. You may find that a motivating factor is also built into the system, and managers may enjoy a bonus based on their performance against the budget.

Integrating Functional/Operational Budgets

Budgets are drawn up for individual budget centers. This allows an analysis of the costs for each center and also reflects the overall strategy of the organization. It is essential that these functional or operational budgets are integrated; otherwise, problems will arise, such as more products being made than can be sold, or the machinery or labor being unavailable to meet the planned output for the month.

The setting of functional budgets is therefore an iterative process. It is usual to start by establishing the sales budget monthly for the coming year. This will quantify the products or services to be sold and put them in financial terms. Having established the sales budget, attention can be given to the production budget. This will show the quantities needed to meet the demands of the sales budget, and a decision will be made on the inventory levels to be held.

In the next two sections, we demonstrate the first steps toward producing a sales budget and the related production budget. Our simplified structure demonstrates the principles, but in reality the process will be more complex and time consuming than our examples.

Sales Budget

The sales team will predict the quantities to be sold in different geographic areas, as this may affect the price received in overseas markets. The organization may also be offering a range of services and products, so a quantitative budget will be required for each one. The quantitative sales budget will then need to be converted into a financial budget. At this stage, the accountant may work with the sales team to determine whether there are any special taxes or import duties, volume discounts, or similar regulatory requirements that may affect selling prices. At a later stage, the accountants will also have to resolve the problems of foreign exchange rates.

With the sales budget in place, it is then possible to conduct an analysis of the costs that will be incurred on resources to achieve the level of sales. At this stage, the analysis of the costs and the decisions made must be in line with organizational strategy, and the detailed information will include such items as

- number of sales people required and the costs of salaries, cars, and other travelling expenses;
- office space and equipment required;
- commissions paid to agents;
- special promotions and discounts;
- an advertising budget for print, television, and other outlets.

Having given you the scope of the work required, we will go back one stage and show an example of compiling a sales budget from outside the manufacturing sector. In this example, the sales budget needs to be constructed from the availability of certain resources. The example also demonstrates the relationship between strategy and budget development.

Example of Creating a Sales Budget

Ensafe is a consultancy that advises homeowners and commercial organizations how they can make their premises more energy efficient. There is substantial demand for their work, but Ensafe has difficulty in recruiting consultants. Last year was financially successful, and the company has now made the decision to pay higher salaries to consultants to expand their work force.

The company employs commercial premises consultants (CPs) and domestic premises consultants (DPs). The 12 CPs were paid $100,000 last year, and the 8 domestic premises (DP) consultants were paid $80,000 last year. Travel and related expenses for the consultants averages 20% of salaries. The cost of running the general office is $140,000 per annum.

The revenue is based on billable hours, and all consultants are expected to bill for 1,500 hours. The rate charge for CPs is $100 per hour and for DP consultants, $70 per hour. The income statement for last year is shown in Table 3.3.

Table 3.3. Income Statement

Revenue	$
CP fees (1,500 hours × 12 × $100)	1,800,000
DP fees (1,500 hours × 8 × $70)	840,000
Total revenue	2,640,000
Costs	**$**
CP consultants' salaries	1,200,000
DP consultants' salaries	640,000
Travel and related expenses	368,000
General office expenses	140,000
Total costs	2,348,000
Profit	**292,000**

Ensafe is considering an increase in all salaries by 10% and recruiting two more CP and three more DP consultants. It is expected that office expenses will increase by 5%. Ensafe is preparing the budget for next year and wishes to make a profit of $350,000 minimum.

The first stage that Ensafe needs to do is to calculate the budget for the total costs. To this they add the target profit to arrive at the revenue figure of $3,507,000. You will note that Ensafe has drawn up the financial statements to the nearest thousand dollars, which is the usual practice unless greater detail is required. In the budget in Table 3.4, the fees for the consultants have been calculated using the additional consultants but retaining the hourly billable rate.

Table 3.4 confirms that to achieve a profit of $350,000, revenue of $3,507,000 is required. Even with the increased number of consultants, the budgeted revenue is only $3,255,000. Merely increasing the number of consultants will not achieve the targeted profit. Ensafe may have to increase its billable rate per hour, but first the company needs to determine its strategy and what the market will accept. This will raise questions on whether the company intends to concentrate on domestic residences or commercial premises. The company also needs to assess the availability of consultants and whether the salaries being offered are sufficient inducement.

Budgets both contribute toward the development of strategy and reflect the financial implication of budget proposals. It is impossible for

Table 3.4. Ensafe Budget

	Actual (thousands of dollars)		Budget (thousands of dollars)
Revenue			
CP fees (1,500 hours × 12 × $100)	1,800	CP fees (1,500 hours × 14 × $100)	2,100
DP fees (1,500 hours × 8 × $70)	840	DP fees (1,500 hours × 11 × $70)	1,155
Total revenue	2,640	Total revenue	3,507
Costs		Costs	
CP consultants' salaries	1,200	CP salaries (14 × $110,000)	1,540
DP consultants' salaries	640	DP salaries (11 × $88,000)	968
Travel and related expenses	368	Travel and related expenses	502
General office expenses	140	General office expenses	147
Total costs	2,348	Total costs	3,157
Profit	292	Profit	350

Ensafe to prepare a credible budget without a strategy and also impossible to adopt a strategy without knowing the financial consequences.

Production Budget

Having considered the consultancy business, we return to a manufacturing organization to demonstrate the calculation of a production budget. The production manager will use the sales budget as the starting base, but a decision will need to be made to determine the amount of inventory that will be held.

Example of Creating a Production Budget

Tapcov starts a new business to manufacture covers in three sizes for cars, motorbikes, and other items. The production manager has been given the quantitative sales for the first 3 months of the year. He is also told that sales are expected to be 10,000 in Month 4. It is also agreed that he will have a closing inventory at the end of each month of 10% of the sales units for the following month.

You should have no difficulty in understanding that the production run in Month 1 must include the closing inventory to form the opening inventory of the next month. In Month 2, we have a total demand of 5,800, but as there are 500 units in inventory, the production requirement is 5,300 units.

Having worked out the quantities to be produced, these now need to be translated into financial terms. The production manager or the accountant may do this, and we will assume that these are the figures used:

Table 3.5. Tapcov Quantitative Production Budgets: Quarter 1

	Month 1	Month 2	Month 3
Sales (given)	5,000	5,000	8,000
Closing inventory at 10% of following month	500	800	1,000
Monthly requirement	5,500	5,800	9,000
Less beginning inventory	0	500	800
Production units required	5,500	5,300	8,200

- *Materials.* Each cover requires 2 meters of material priced at $1.50 per meter.
- *Labor.* Five covers can be made in one hour at the labor rate of $10.00 per hour.

In Table 3.6, we have considered only the direct costs. The production manager now has the problem of determining the overheads for the department—the indirect costs. There may be supervisors' salaries, maintenance costs, and depreciation of machinery all specific to that department. The production manager can also expect that a share of the factory overheads will also be allocated to the budget. These probably will be uncontrollable as far as the production manager is concerned.

Even with this simple budget you will realize that both the procurement manager for the supply of materials and the department responsible for employment of workers must be involved. There is also the funding for machinery and the acquisition of other resources to be resolved. You will also appreciate that the more detailed the information, the better will be the analysis. There can be a tendency to concentrate on the direct production costs such as materials and labor with insufficient effort spent on the analysis of overhead costs and how these support the organizational strategy.

Because of the complexity and time taken in setting budgets, there are criticisms of the technique. But you will appreciate how it coordinates the activities of managers in the achievement of the strategic purpose of the organization. Also, regular monthly reporting of the actual performance against the budget will allow managers to take corrective action and discuss with colleagues the implications for their own departments.

Table 3.6. Production Budget: Quarter 1

	Month 1	Month 2	Month 3
Production units required	5,500	5,300	8,200
Material cost ($)	16,500	15,900	24,600
Labor cost ($)	*11,000*	*10,600*	*16,400*
Total direct costs ($)	27,500	26,500	41,000
Overheads ($)	?	?	?

Conclusions

Financial planning is a critical aspect of strategy. In this chapter, we have explained the development of standard costs and of budgets. Standard costing is widely used in manufacturing, particularly for direct costs. We have discussed how standards should be developed from valid sources of information so that the standards have credibility. We have also indicated how standard costing is used as a basis of identifying possible reasons for actual direct costs to differ from the standard. These differences are known as variances, and we explain the calculation and interpretation of these in the next chapter.

Budgetary control is a major financial planning exercise and completely wedded to corporate strategy. We have described the different approaches that companies have and these are

- top-down budgets imposed by senior management,
- bottom-up budgets where all managers participate at an early stage,
- scenario planning that attempts to predict the future environment the company will operate in and allows managers to generate budgets within these parameters.

There are different methods for developing budgets:

- Incremental budgeting is where the new budget is set by adding or deducting an incremental percentage to either the current year's actual income and expenditure or the present budget.
- Zero-base budgeting is where each manager develops his or her own budget but must justify the presence and costs of all activities assuming a zero base.
- Rolling budgets can take many forms, but usually prior or present actual performance is used as a basis for setting budgets for near-future performance.
- Activity-based budgets are like a reversal of ABC, and attention is given to the costs of activities that are used to produce and sell products and services, rather than the functional department costs.

Toward the end of this chapter, we considered the procedural aspects of budgeting and the systems and committees required to implement a budget. We would emphasize that the process is extremely time consuming, and unless the budgets have credibility, managers can become disillusioned. We also used examples to demonstrate the development of budgets and their integration.

Planning is the part of strategic cost analysis that is embedded in the development of corporate strategy. It is impossible to develop budgets without a corporate strategy or to generate corporate strategy without budgets. In the next chapter, we look at standard costing and budgets from the aspect of monitoring and control of actual performance—strategy in action.

CHAPTER 4

Monitoring and Control

About This Chapter

Control is a feedback system that covers both the action that implements the strategic decisions and the performance evaluation of personnel and operations. As a manager, you use feedback from financial performance reports that you normally receive at least monthly but possibly weekly, or even in real time. These reports may have different titles, but for your managerial responsibilities, the reports show the organization's financial plan for a period, the actual performance achieved, and the difference between the two, which is called the variance.

You use the performance report specific to your responsibilities to identify activities that are not conforming to the organization's plan and not contributing to its strategy. You conduct management by exception by investigating these differences between the plan and actual performance. The cost analysis helps you to determine your effectiveness and efficiency on implementing business strategies and to decide whether corrective action is necessary.

The two main techniques used to analyze departures from the plan are standard costing and budgetary control, which were discussed in the previous chapter. We looked at determining our strategic objectives and building those into financial plans to be used by managers. Once the plans have been established, control is maintained by comparing actual against planned performance. In this chapter, you will learn how to use the reports arising from the application of standard costing and budgetary control techniques to conduct an in-depth analysis of the performance reports you receive.

Standard Cost Variances

Any analysis benefits from detailed, accurate, and timely information. A thorough appraisal of standard cost variances can provide many benefits. However, the analysis is not completed by the mere calculation of differences between actual and planned performance but by an investigation as to why they arose and the decisions that need to be made that correspond with existing strategy or a reappraisal of that strategy.

One of the advantages of standard cost variances is that they are interrelated. You can calculate variances for a full range of activities, and the sum of these variances will demonstrate the impact of the variances on the planned profit. A hard financial number demonstrates strategic success or failure.

Depending on the nature of the organization, there are many variances that can be calculated. We are going to limit our discussions to two direct cost variances, two overhead variances, and a sales variance. These examples will explain the basic principles.

Direct Cost Variances

Direct Materials Variances

The direct material variances seek to answer the question whether the *actual* total cost of the direct materials for a certain level of production is the same as you planned. More importantly, you are guided to the probable reasons for any differences, and you can place these in a strategic context.

As explained in the previous chapter, the total cost of materials is made up by the amount of materials you use and the price you pay. Predetermined standards are set for both the usage level of direct materials for a given level of production and the price allowed per unit of direct materials.

The reason for the actual total cost of direct material differing from the plan is either we paid more or less per unit of materials than we planned or we used more or less materials than we planned. This could be due to poor planning, a change in market conditions that may require a new strategic approach, or a deviation from the original strategy.

The relationship between usage and price, and the formulas we use can be shown in a diagrammatic form:

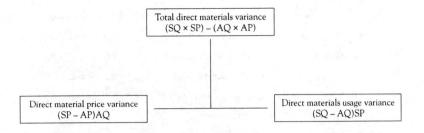

$$SQ = \text{standard quantity used}$$
$$SP = \text{standard price per unit}$$
$$AQ = \text{actual quantity used}$$
$$AP = \text{actual price per unit.}$$

This can be demonstrated by a simple example. A company is making leather luggage cases, and they set the following standards of materials for their "flight carry-on model": 1.5 meters at $5.00 per meter. In 1 month, 500 cases were produced and the actual costs incurred were $3,496 for 760 meters of leather that were used in production. The calculations are as follows.

Total Direct Materials Variance
$$(SQ \times SP) - (AQ \times AP) = (750 \text{ meters} \times \$5) - (\$3,496) =$$
$$\$3,750 - \$3,496 = \$254F$$

Direct Material Price Variance
$$(SP - AP)AQ$$
$$(\$5.00 - \$4.60) \times 760 = \$304F$$

Material Usage Variance
$$(SQ - AQ)SP$$
$$(750 - 760) \times \$5 = \$50U$$

Just a note on the calculations before we explain the variances and their relationships: We were not given the actual price per meter of material, so we divided the total cost of $3,496 by the total usage of 760 meters to obtain the actual price per meter of $4.60. You will find that in a computerized system, all these calculations will be done, but it is useful for you to be able to understand the basis of the calculations.

Now let us look at the variances. As we have observed before, the variance is the difference between the standard and the actual. If your performance is better than the standard, you have a favorable variance. If it is worse than the standard, you have an unfavorable variance. When we use the term favorable and unfavorable, this refers to the impact of the actual performance on the planned profit.

In the formulas, we have a favorable total direct materials variance of $254F, and if there are no other variances with other direct costs, our actual profit for the period will be $254 higher than we planned. What we want to know is the reason for this improved performance, and the reasons are given in the two subvariances. We have a favorable price variance of $304 and $50 unfavorable for the usage variance. If you net these off, you get the overall favorable variance of $254.

Further investigation is required to explain these variances. One plausible reason is that an inferior quality material was purchased at a lower price than planned. However, this poor quality led to greater wastage and thus the unfavorable usage variance. There could, of course, be other reasons, but you will find it useful to relate the variable to each other and not only consider them in isolation.

In carrying out your investigations, it is essential to pay attention to the strategic context. Has the company decided on a cost reduction strategy, or is it aiming at producing a high-quality item. The overall material variance may be favorable when considered in isolation, but how do the individual components relate to the organization's strategy?

In the previous example, we demonstrated the material usage variance: the actual quantity of materials used in the production of that number of cases. Some companies calculate a materials-purchased variance, as this is the responsibility of the purchasing manager, and the production manager is only responsible for the usage of the materials.

Direct Labor Variances

In calculating the direct labor variances, we use the same principles for material variances. Some companies will refer to this variance as the wage rate variance. As with materials, the reason for the actual total cost of direct labor differing from the plan is either we paid more or less per hour for labor than we planned or we required more or less labor hours than we had planned for that level of production.

The terms we use for the subvariances are direct labor rate—that is, how much we paid per hour—and direct labor efficiency variance (sometimes referred to as the labor productivity variance). This is the difference between the actual production achieved, measured in standard hours, and the actual hours worked, valued at the standard labor rate.

The relationship between these events and the formulas we use can be shown in a diagrammatic form:

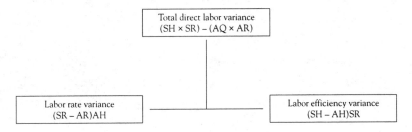

SH = standard hours

SR = standard rate per hour

AH = actual number of hours worked

AR = actual rate per hour.

We use the same example as before. A company is making leather luggage cases and has set the following labor standards for their "flight carry-on model." Labor is expected to make 2 cases each hour, and the wage rate is $12 per hour.

In 1 month, 500 cases were produced, and the actual costs incurred were $11.50 per hour for 280 hours of work. The calculations are as follows.

Total Direct Labor Variance

$$(SH \times SR) - (AH \times AR) = (250 \text{ hours} \times \$12) - (280 \text{ hours} \times \$11.50) =$$
$$\$3,000 - \$3,220 = \$220U$$

Labor Rate Variance

$$(SR - AR)AH = (\$12 \times \$11.50) \, 280 = \$140F$$

Labor Efficiency Variance

$$(SH - AH)SR = (250 - 280) \times \$12 = \$360U$$

You can see that the unfavorable labor rate variance is explained by a favorable rate variance of $140F (we paid less per hour than planned) and an unfavorable efficiency variance of $360.

One plausible explanation is that we employed labor that was less skilled at a lower hourly rate, and therefore they took longer to do the work. Of course, you should always place any variance in the context of any related variance, in this case the materials used. On the face of it, inferior materials may have been used, so it is plausible that workers took longer because of the difficulty in working with the poor quality materials.

The variances give you signposts to direct your investigations. If there are no variances, then you can practice "management by exception" and take no action. But remember that both favorable and unfavorable variances should be investigated. Toward the end of this chapter, we give advice on techniques that permit you to concentrate your attention where it is most needed.

Overhead Variances

In some companies, the standard costing system may be expanded to monitor and control indirect costs as well as direct costs. This is usually restricted to production overheads and is most useful where it is possible to analyze the budgeted and actual production overheads into their fixed and variable cost elements. You will realize that this aspect of variance analysis is closely linked to full or absorption costing where overheads are recovered. It also concentrates on activity levels and is therefore concerned with the utilization of capacity.

This area of analysis is frequently left to the accountant to investigate, as it relates to the budget setting for indirect costs and the decision on how they will be charged to production. In many organizations, the overhead cost is usually very significant and is a keystone of strategy formulation. It may be that in your career you will never encounter overhead variances but the following explanation provides a general foundation if you are taking a broader strategic perspective.

Variable Overhead Variances

We are continuing the principles established for the direct cost variances, but the terminology changes. A main variance is calculated and analyzed by two subvariances, as shown in the following diagram, assuming that the labor hour rate is used for charging overheads to production:

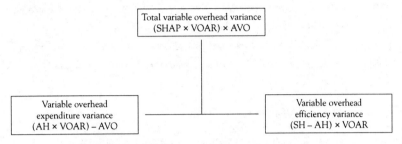

SHAP = standard hours for the actual number of units produced
VOAR = variable overhead absorption rate
AVO = actual variable overhead incurred
AH = actual hours worked.

Example of Variable Overhead Variances
A company budgets its variable overheads for the period as $21,000, and it plans to produce 1,500 units with a standard labor time of 5 hours per unit. For the financial period, it produced 1,650 units. Its actual variable overhead cost is $20,000, and the actual hours worked were 8,500 hours.

The first stage is to calculate the standard hours allowed for the number of units actually produced (SHAP). This is 1,650 units × 5 hours per unit = 8,250 hours. The second calculation is the allocation rate that is based on labor hours. The standard labor hours are 1,500 × 5 = 7,500 hours. The predetermined allocation rate is therefore the budgeted overhead divided by the planned hours: $21,000 / 7,500 = $2.80.

Total Variable Overhead Variance
(SHAP × VOAR) − AVO = (8,250 × $2.80) − $20,000 =
$23,100 − $20,000 = $3,100F

Variable Overhead Expenditure Variance
(AH × VOAR) − AVO = (8,500 × $2.80) − $20,000 =
$23,800 − $20,000 = $3,800F

Variable Overhead Efficiency Variance
$$(\text{SHAP} - \text{AH}) \times \text{VOAR} = (8{,}250 - 8{,}500)\ \$2.80 = 250 \times \$2.80 =$$
$$\$700\text{U}$$

After interpreting these calculations, we can see that the favorable total overhead variance of $3,100 favorable comprises two elements. The variable overhead expenditure variance shows that we only spent $20,000 on variable overheads, although the amount calculated for this level of production was $23,800. However, more labor hours were actually used than planned, and this resulted in an unfavorable variance of $700.

Fixed Overhead Variances

In looking at fixed overhead variances, you must bear in mind that we are assuming that these overheads will remain the same regardless of changes in activity. We are still going to be concerned whether the total amount of actual fixed overhead is the same as we planned. Efficiency is not an issue, but what is important is whether we used the capacity at our disposal to the extent that we planned, and this is known as the volume variance. In diagrammatic form, the variances are as follows:

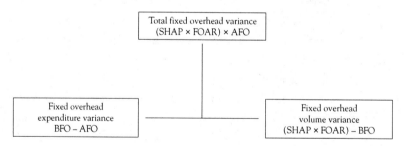

SHAP = standard hours for the actual number of units produced
AFO = actual fixed overhead incurred
FOAR = budgeted fixed overheads allocation rate
BFO = budgeted fixed overheads.

Example of Fixed Overhead Variances
A company budgets its fixed overheads for the period as $16,500, and it plans to produce 1,500 units with a standard labor time of 5 hours per unit. For the financial period, it produced 1,650 units. Its actual fixed

overhead cost is $15,000, and the actual hours worked were 8,500 hours. The calculation of standard hours from the actual number of units produced is 1,650 × 5 hours = 8,250 hours.

Assuming that we are using the labor hours as an allocation base for the fixed overhead, the calculation of the fixed overhead allocation rate is planned fixed overheads divided by planned labor hours. That is $16,500 / 7,500 = $2.20.

Total Fixed Overhead Variance
$$(SHAP \times FOAR) - AFO = (8,250 \times \$2.20) - \$15,000 =$$
$$\$18,150 - \$15,000 = \$3,150F$$

Fixed Overhead Expenditure Variance
$$(BFO - AFO) = (\$16,500 - \$15,000) = \$1,500F$$

Fixed Overhead Volume Variance
$$(SHAP \times FOAR) - BFO = (\$18,150 - \$16,500) = \$1,650F$$

The total fixed overhead is easy to understand if you remember full or absorption costing. At the beginning of the financial period, we calculated that we would charge $2.20 for every standard labor hour. The number of units produced (1,650) should have been completed in 8,250 labor hours. We therefore charged $18,150 for fixed overheads during the year, but as the actual overheads were only $15,000, we have a favorable variance of $3,150. One reason for this is that our actual fixed overheads were lower than our planned fixed overheads by $1,500—a favorable variance. Our fixed overhead volume variance of $1,650 favorable arises because we charged $18,150 to production for fixed overheads instead of the budget of $16,500 as our activity was higher than planned.

Sales Variances

Unfortunately, some companies pay too much attention to production cost variances and ignore sales variances. These are critical to the strategic management of any organization, and if you are in the sales function you need to understand these variances. There are several sales variances that can be calculated, such as sales price, sales volume, sales mix, sales quantity, market size, and market share variances.

In this section, we are going to concentrate on sales margin variances. However, you should be cautious in selecting the variances you need for your decision making and their interpretation. Using different bases for the calculation could give different results. The sales margin variance is widely used possibly because it generates variances that relate to the impact of the quantities sold and the prices charged. It is referred to as a sales *margin* variance, as it uses the profit margin in the calculations. The variances are as follows:

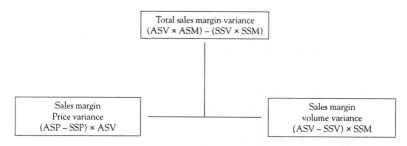

ASV = actual sales volume
ASM = actual sales margin
SSV = standard sales volume
SSM = standard sales margin
ASP = actual sales price
SSP = standard sales price.

Example of Sales Margin Variance
A company establishes a standard selling price of $15 per unit for its product. The standard for the direct costs per unit is $4.40 and for production overheads $5.40 per unit. The total standard cost is therefore $9.80 to give a standard margin of $5.20. In the financial period, the company plans to sell 5,000 units of its main product. Ultimately, it actually sold 5,400 units at $14.00 per unit, and the actual cost was $9.00 per unit.

Total Sales Margin

$$(ASV \times ASM) - (SSV \times SSM) = (5,400 \times \$5.00) - (5,000 \times \$5.20) =$$
$$(\$27,000 - \$26,000) = \$1,000F$$

Sales Margin Price Variance
   $(ASM - SSM) \times ASV = (\$5.00 - \$5.20) \times 5,400 = \$1.080A$

Sales Margin Volume Variance
   $(ASV - SSV) \times SSM = (5,400 - 5,000) \times \$5.20 = \$2080F$

The analysis reveals that by reducing the selling price you get an adverse variance of $1,080. The reduction in the selling price and the change in actual costs result in a reduced sales margin of $5.00 per unit, but the significant increase in the volume sold gives a sales margin volume variance of $2,080F.

You will appreciate that, in using the sales margin, the relationship between the production costs and the selling price becomes critical. Although this example is simplified, it emphasizes that any strategic decisions on cost, volumes, and selling price cannot be made without the relevant data. Standard costing provides that information.

Budget Variances

Identifying Variances

As you might expect, the actual performance of an organization will not correspond entirely with the original budgets as the year progresses. As with standard costing, there will be differences between planned and actual performance. Where the actual differs from the budget, there will be either an adverse or an unfavorable variance. Where the actual costs are lower than the budget, there will be a favorable variance. With sales, the reverse is true. If actual sales are higher than the budget, the variance is favorable; if lower, the variance is adverse.

Similar to standard costing, a budget is determined to be unfavorable or favorable due to its impact on the budgeted profit. If your actual costs are $10,000 higher than planned costs, this will mean that your budget profit is hit by the $10,000. If your sales are $5,000 lower than planned, then your actual profit will be unfavorably affected compared to your budget.

Unlike standard costing, we do not have a hierarchy of formulas to assist us in our investigations, so you must be able to appreciate the relationship of the variances. As manager, you will normally receive a budget report monthly comparing your department's actual performance against the budget. The report you receive will most likely be a "line-by-line" budget and will show the planned amount for the month, the actual, and the variance. Some reports may also show the same information for the year to date.

Table 4.1 shows the performance for 1 month. This budget report has only seven lines of information, and you can expect to see budgets with many more items identified.

We do not know whether this is a merchandising company that buys goods from suppliers and then sells them, or if it is a manufacturer. It does not matter! The key message when looking at this budget is that the month was a disaster. We budgeted for a profit of $50,000, but the actual profit was only $10,000 due to aggregate variances of $40,000 unfavorable. If the company has a strategy, it needs urgent treatment before it expires completely.

As a manager, it will be your responsibility to identify the main issues and to take action. To do this, you will need to identify which are the important variances, and "management by exception" is widely used. In other words, you investigate those variances that are exceptional, usually because of their size. However, this is not the only way.

In the next section, we will explain a more sophisticated approach than just using monthly "dollar" size as a measure. But first, let us improve the budget report in Table 4.1 to make it more helpful. One adjustment is to add a line to show "Gross Profit." This is the difference between the

Table 4.1. Monthly Budget

	Budget (thousands of dollars)	Actual (thousands of dollars)	Variance (thousands of dollars)
Revenue	965	978	13F
Cost of goods sold	(650)	(667)	17U
Salaries	(120)	(105)	15F
Administration overheads	(20)	(38)	18U
Distribution	(35)	(32)	3F
Selling overheads	(90)	(126)	36U
Profit	50	10	40U

cost to you of the goods you sell or manufacture and the price you receive for them. It is a key indicator of performance.

The second adjustment will be to add a final column to show the percentage impact of the variance. We have calculated the figures by expressing the variance as a percentage of the budget. Some organizations prefer to use the actual, and some will calculate the variance as a percentage of the budgeted or actual profit. You need to ascertain the practice in your own organization. The adjusted report is shown in Table 4.2.

One figure still missing is the quantity of items sold, and we will examine the value of this information when we consider flexible budgets in the next chapter.

Before looking more closely at some of these figures, let us tackle the easier items. A saving of $15,000 (12.5%) is made on salaries. If you are a good manager, you should already know the events that led to this and made the appropriate decisions.

Administration overheads show a substantial unfavorable variance in both the dollar amount and the percentage. Once again, you should be already aware of the background. One possible scenario is that you are unable to hire full-time employees and resort to outsourcing or other support mechanisms, which is coded into the administration overheads. Check on this!

Table 4.2. Adjusted Monthly Budget Report

	Budget (thousands of dollars)	Actual (thousands of dollars)	Variance (thousands of dollars)	Variance (%)
Revenue	965	978	13F	1.35 F
Cost of goods sold	(650)	(667)	17U	2.62U
Gross profit	**315 (32.6%)**	**311 (31.8%)**	**4U**	
Salaries	(120)	(105)	15F	12.5F
Administration overheads	(20)	(38)	18U	90.0U
Distribution	(35)	(32)	3F	8.57F
Selling overheads	(90)	(126)	36U	40.0U
Profit	50	10	40U	80.0U

The most intriguing combination of variances revolves around the revenue and cost of sales figures. Although the variances are not large, you should always be alert to changes that directly affect gross profit. As the percentage gross profit has declined, this suggests several different scenarios, two of which are typical:

1. Your costs have increased, so you have increased your selling price but insufficiently to maintain your gross margin.
2. You have reduced your selling price, and your volume of sales has increased, but this increase in volume has led to higher cost of goods sold.

The substantial increase in selling overheads indicates a push on sales, but the saving on distribution costs suggests that there has not been an increase in volume. These are intriguing questions, and all of them reflect the financial implications of the strategies that you have pursued during the month.

In this simple example, we have only been able to speculate on reasons for the variances, and as a manager you should be so familiar with the activities for which you have a responsibility that you know where to carry out your investigations. So the variances are operating as signposts, but with a much more comprehensive budget, you need some guidelines to know how to apply "management by exception." We discuss this in the next section.

Investigating Variances

As a manager, you should be monitoring activities in your department and identifying where things are going well or poorly. Both favorable and unfavorable variance should be investigated. The budget report will give you the financial consequences of these occurrences and also illuminate some aspects that would not otherwise be apparent. It also allows you to concentrate your attention on where the financial impact is important. There are several ways to identify the variances you should investigate.

Dollars and Percentages

One way to measure the importance of the variance is to set limits on the differences and any variance outside that limit you investigate. You might set as a general rule that any variance $20,000 over or under the budgeted figure will be investigated. If we apply this rule to the previous example, only the selling overheads will be investigated. Similarly, if we use only percentages, we would miss important issues. The way to resolve this dilemma is to use both dollars and percentages. You would therefore investigate any variance that deviated by either $20,000 *or* 10%.

Even that could result in some important areas missing investigation, so we will explain how you can improve your analytical abilities.

Recurring Variances

Variances may fall within the boundaries you have set, so on a month-by-month basis you may not feel concerned. What you must be alert to is the situation where a variance is occurring repeatedly for the same item. Based on the data in Table 4.2, we give the first 3 months' variances for distribution costs in Table 4.3.

Although the variance for each month falls within our limits, it is worrying that each month shows a variance. This is a favorable variance and in dollars. We are not looking at substantial amounts, but the percentage is hovering close to our 10% time after time. It would be worth looking at this variance to ascertain the reason.

The first move would be to look at the original budget and to see whether it appears credible, particularly as the organization may have increased its sales volume. You will often find that in your investigations you need to consider the entire strategic demands of the entire activity. If the budget seems credible, the next question may be whether new and more efficient procedures have been introduced. If so, let us see

Table 4.3. Monthly Variances: Distribution Costs

Month	Variance ($)	Variance (%)
January	3,000F	8.57F
February	2,500F	7.24F
March	2,800F	7.85F

whether we can improve them further or apply them in other parts of the organization.

If, after pursuing the above lines of inquiry and any others you can identify, there is no obvious answer, a deeper delve may be necessary. We mentioned in the previous chapter about the relationships between budgets and behavior. Some managers like to "beat their budgets" and may find devious ways to do so. Ignoring maintenance, losing invoices, using inferior materials, and infringing regulations are just some of the ways. As a manager you would have to consider the possibility that subordinates may be adopting unacceptable practices.

Trends

In this example we are going to apply our limits of $20,000 and 10% again but use new data. Let us assume that for maintenance costs in the factory, the variances for 3 months are as shown in Table 4.4.

Although comfortably under our budget limits, this variance is increasing each month. You do not want this to blow up in your face sometime in June or even earlier. If you see the trend of a variance increasing or decreasing over a period of time, you need to investigate.

Control Charts

The degree of sophistication you apply to these can differ from the visual to the statistical. As a busy manager, you sometimes need to focus on a few key budget figures. You may find it useful to show these in a chart form and plot the data over a period of time. This can be useful on your office wall or can form part of a presentation. The example in Figure 4.1 plots the variance for the total departmental costs over a 6-month period.

Table 4.4. Monthly Variance

Month	Variance ($)	Variance (%)
January	12,000U	6.5U
February	14,500U	7.0U
March	15,500U	7.3U

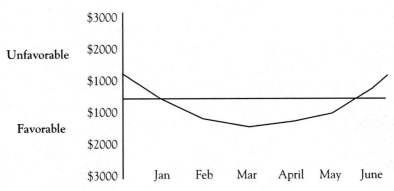

Figure 4.1. Visual control chart.

In Figure 4.1, it appears as if the manager reversed an unfavorable January and established increasingly favorable variances until March. Performance then commenced to June when it again entered the unfavorable zone. The reasons for this unfavorable variance need to be investigated. The manager could also add lines to indicate where investigations should commence or plot the standard deviations.

Contradictions and Anomalies

The final method suggested is easier for the experienced manager, but all managers should be thinking along these lines, with the feeling that "something is not right" when you look at your monthly budget report. Possibly you know that certain costs have increased, but an unfavorable variance against budget is not being shown. Why not? You may have introduced more efficient processes and procedures, but a favorable variance is not being shown. Why not?

In some instances, it is the relationship between various activities as reflected in the budgets that generates a contradiction. In Figure 4.1, the sales revenue increased. We do not know whether that was an increase due to price or volume, but if it is the latter, you would have expected the distribution costs to also increase.

In this section, we looked at the variances arising from comparing the actual performance against the static or fixed budget. Several of our comments are based on the fact that the static budget is set at the beginning of the financial period, and no changes are made to it during the period. For an organization in a stable environment, this is a good approach because it gives certainty and a clear direction toward the strategic objectives.

But what if the environment changes during the financial period, and there are variations in activity? You would expect the actual performance to be different from the static budget. This difficulty is resolved by the flexible budget that we explain in our next section.

Flexible Budgets

Fluctuating Activity

The discussions in the preceding section concerned static, or fixed, budgets. These are set at the beginning of the year and are not changed merely because the actual activity levels differ from the budget activity. If there are significant changes in the environment, or the organization amends its strategic plan, changes may then be made. Static budgets are appropriate where activity levels are consistent or are controllable by the manager.

A major drawback of static budgets is that an unfavorable variance can arise in *variable* cost variances because of a beneficial increase in activity levels. For example, actual sales volume may be higher than planned because of a buoyant market. This growth in sales volume will cause an increase in actual production and distribution costs to support the sales. With a fixed budget, these will show as unfavorable variances although the overall organizational performance is good.

This problem can be resolved by using a flexible budget where activity levels fluctuate and are uncontrollable by the manager responsible. The flexing of the budget refers only to variable costs and if there is a cost variance it can be assumed to be due to an increase or decrease in activity.

The Flexed Budget

The usual procedure is to set the budget at the beginning of the period for the planned level of activity. At the end of the month, the variable costs in the budget are then adjusted in line with the actual level of activity achieved. Fixed costs are not normally flexed as they should remain the same regardless of any changes in activity within the relevant range.

In Table 4.5, we compare a static and flexible budget. The static budget was set for 40,000 units to be produced and sold. At the end of the month, the actual number of units produced and sold is 45,000. The static budget is then flexed, and the results are shown in the next column. The actual performance is then compared with the flexed budget to give the variance in the final column.

The calculation of the flexed budget is the total budgeted sales or cost amount divided by the budgeted number of units. The resulting budgeted amount per unit is then multiplied by the actual number of units for the financial period.

First, a comment on the revenue. For the same number of units, we managed to obtain $3,000 more than the flexible budget. So our volume increased, but our total actual sales is higher than our flexed budget. This

Table 4.5. Static and Flexible Budgets Compared

	Static budget	Flexible budget	Actual performance	Variance
Number of units	40,000	45,000	45,000	
Revenue ($5.00 per unit in thousands of dollars)	200	225	228	3F
Variable costs				
Direct materials (1.20 per unit in thousands of dollars)	48	54	62	8U
Direct labor (1.60 per unit in thousands of dollars)	64	72	67	5F
Variable overheads ($0.40 in thousands of dollars)	16	18	17	1F
Fixed overheads				
Lighting and heat (in thousands of dollars)	15	15	16	1U
Depreciation (in thousands of dollars)	23	23	23	
Insurance (in thousands of dollars)	26	26	31	5U
Profit (in thousands of dollars)	8	17	12	5U

suggests that there has been a small price increase. This could have been a strategic decision or merely an opportunistic action.

Next, the variable costs. If we had compared our actual variable costs to the original static budget, all items would have shown an unfavorable variance because production was higher than originally planned. Comparing to our flexible budget, we see that only direct materials gives an unfavorable variance. The variance is not large, but it may be worth investigating. One plausible reason may be that a better quality of material was used, and this may also explain the slight increase in the selling price. Once again, the question arises whether this is in line with strategy.

Fixed overheads should have remained the same, but the one to investigate is insurance. It is possible that the original quote was not correct, or additional items were insured that were not in the original quote.

The aforementioned example suggests that flexible budgeting is far superior, as it results in more credible budgets. However, there are disadvantages. The production manager has planned originally to manufacture 200,000 units but is called upon to increase this by 25,000 units. This means more materials have to be ordered, more labor may be required, and there may not be sufficient capacity on the machinery, so overtime has to be worked. In other words, the planned coordination of activities can be disrupted. If there is a strong strategy underpinning these actions, there is no problem, and proper coordination of all the activities should have been achieved.

There is also a problem if actual activity levels are lower than planned. As the variable costs will be flexed, there may be no unfavorable variances. The managers in those departments may be very satisfied with the performance of their own areas of responsibility, but at the organizational level it may be a disaster. Managers are individually responsible for their own areas but are also collectively responsible for the organizational performance and adherence to the strategy. Flexible budgets may distract from that collective approach to achieving the strategic goals.

Budgeting Assessed

The Strengths

In the previous chapter, we explained the relationship between strategic objectives and budgeting and described budgeting procedures, the inter-relationships of budgeting, and the use of budgets as monitoring and control mechanisms. Budgetary control has many strengths, and there are potential advantages to an organization using the technique:

- The strategic goals of the organization are translated into detailed financial plans.
- A coherent system of monitoring and control is established.
- The identification of budget centers structures the responsibilities of managers for identified activities.
- Integration of the various parts of the organization takes place.
- Managers are motivated by the clarification of objectives, the performance expected, and the reporting of progress.
- The analysis of variances allows managers to take timely corrective action where necessary.
- Where actual activity fluctuates, flexible budgets provide a method for relating variable costs to these changes.

The Weaknesses

Although budgetary control is widely used, there are some potential drawbacks even with a well-managed system:

- Establishing budgets is a time-consuming process.
- If static budgets are used and activity fluctuates, the reported variances will have no credibility.
- Managers can become demotivated if they consider the budgets are unrealistic.
- Once managers realize that they will meet their budget amounts, there is little incentive to work harder.
- The system may encourage dysfunctional work behavior, as discussed in the previous chapter.

- It is a complex process requiring skills in both setting plans and implementing them in the organization.
- Budgets emphasize central control that may inhibit managerial initiative.
- In a turbulent environment, the assumption that the long term future can be predicted and activities driven by these plans may not be viable.

Conclusions

In this chapter, we demonstrated how you can monitor and control actual performance. This is achieved by comparing your actual performance against your standards or budgets for the financial period and investigating the variances. If you performed better than planned, you will have a favorable variance; if worse than planned, an unfavorable variance.

The first part of the chapter examined standard cost variances. The basic principle underpinned all the calculations, and we demonstrated

- using material price variance to investigate differences due to the actual price for materials being different from the plan,
- using material usage variance to investigate differences due to the actual quantity of materials used in production being different from the plan,
- using labor rate variance to investigate differences due to the actual rate paid to labor being different from the plan,
- using labor efficiency variance to investigate differences due to more or less work completed than was allowed for in the planned time.

We also explained overhead expenditure variance and the overhead volume variance, although these are usually of greater interest to the accountant than the general manager. Sales margin variances were also explained, and these can be of critical importance. You need to take care in defining and interpreting this variance.

With budget variances, we explained how to identify the variances and gave the following guidelines to determine which variances you need to investigate:

- Dollar amounts or percentage guidelines can be set so that you investigate any variance outside these boundaries.
- Recurring variances may not be large, but if they continue month after month, they should be investigated.
- Trends, either favorable or unfavorable, should be watched. If a variance is gradually increasing or decreasing month after month, you should examine it in order to avoid a future problem.
- Contradictions and anomalies are likely to arise, and as a manager, you should be alert to any variances that do not match your personal observations or your experience.

Budgetary control is a time-consuming process, and we completed the chapter by reflecting on its strengths and weaknesses. We also discussed the criticisms made of the technique. Despite the issues concerning the application and maintenance of the system, few companies would abandon it completely, as it is so entwined with corporate strategy. The explanations and guidance in this chapter may assist in you ensuring that you gain the maximum benefits from the technique.

CHAPTER 5

Managerial Decision Making

About This Chapter

In this chapter, you will encounter a group of techniques designed to provide managers with tools to make decisions among different alternatives, using decision criteria. These techniques are based on the classification of costs in chapter 2. The assumption is that, at least in the short term, costs classified as fixed will stay the same over a period of time irrespective of changes in the level of activity. On the other hand, variable costs will change in direct proportion to fluctuations in levels of activity. In this chapter, we concentrate on fixed and variable cost analysis. In the succeeding chapter, we broaden our scope to examine a range of other decision-making techniques.

There are several stages in decision making. First, specify the problem or opportunity to be investigated, including the financial and nonfinancial constraints. Second, identify feasible alternative options and select the decision model you intend to use. From earlier chapters, you understand the importance of using different costs for different purposes. Finally, aggregate all the relevant information and compare the various options.

The selected option will be based on a cost–benefit analysis and you should recognize any nonfinancial characteristics that may be important from the strategic viewpoint. In other words, when using strategic cost analysis, you must incorporate considerations such as industry structure, market composition, ownership structure, demand and supply variables, interest rates, political changes, inflation or deflation, management compensation, regulatory changes, and globalization.

To enhance management decision making, sensitivity analysis should be used. Different scenarios can be compared to assess the impact of changes, such as interest, prices, and consumer demand that could change the predicted outcomes substantially.

Fluctuating Activity and Costs

Cost Behavior

Very few organizations have the good fortune to be placed in an environment where stability is the norm. Change is a feature of business, whether it be changes in labor costs, material prices, or consumer demand. In this section, we consider what happens to costs when there is a change in activity levels, and we elaborate on the two types of cost behavior that you encountered in chapter 2:

- A variable cost varies in total directly with changes in the level of activity.
- A fixed cost stays the same in total irrespective of changes in the level of activity.

The important features you should note with these definitions are as follows:

- Changes in cost are related solely to activity levels. Costs can change for other reasons, such as increased labor rates.
- The assumptions of change are based on the short-term.
- Activity-level changes, in practice, are within a restricted range.
- Activity levels can be measured by a method that is most appropriate for the organization.

A simple example of a variable cost is material cost. If you are making a product that requires 3 meters of material at $2.00 per meter, your cost for one cost unit is $6.00. If you make 2 units, it is $12.00; 3 units, $18.00; and so on. If you consider period costs, such as rent or insurance, you must pay these whether you are operating at 100% capacity or 5%. These costs are fixed in relation to activity-level changes.

You should have now realized that those costs that are considered direct costs must be variable costs: Those that are indirect will be fixed. But take care! The techniques we explain in this chapter are based on simplifying assumptions that may not hold up in certain economic conditions, certain industries and organizations, and even in your own company.

With that word of caution, Table 5.1 shows you the way that variable, fixed, and total costs are assumed to behave where production activity fluctuates. The normal activity is given as 1,000 units, and at that level, total variable costs are $2,000 and total fixed costs are $5,000.

In this contrived and somewhat dramatic example, you can see the impact of fluctuating activity and the substantial changes in the total cost per unit. It is doubtful that in real life you would encounter such changes, but you can appreciate that with tight margins, a slight decrease in activity will raise your total cost per unit and reduce your profit.

You will also appreciate the reasons for the demand for increased productivity in both the manufacturing and service sectors. In many service companies, the overheads or period costs are high compared to the variable costs, which may only comprise direct labor.

In the example in Table 5.1, we assume that variable costs respond directly and symmetrically to changes in activity levels, whether increasing or decreasing. Research demonstrates that is not the case. A phenomenon has been identified, known as "sticky cost" behavior.

Research has found that costs increase more with activity increases than they decrease in response to equivalent activity decreases. A study of a sample of U.S., UK, French, and German firms revealed that operating costs are sticky in response to changes in revenues.[1] On average, operating costs increase by around 0.97% per 1% increase in revenues, but decrease by only 0.91% per 1% decrease in revenues. The research also concluded that costs tend to be less sticky over longer time horizons and when firms sustain larger drops in revenue.

Table 5.1. Cost Behavior With Fluctuating Activity

Number of units	Variable costs		Fixed costs		Total costs	
	Total ($)	Per unit ($)	Total ($)	Per unit ($)	Total	Per unit
1,000	2,000	2.00	5,000	5.00	7,000	7.00
500	1,000	2.00	5,000	10.00	6,000	12.00
200	400	2.00	5,000	25.00	5,400	27.00
2,000	4,000	2.00	5,000	2.50	9,000	4.50
2,500	5,000	2.00	5,000	2.00	10,000	4.00

Another issue is concerned with payments to labor. The technique assumes that direct labor costs are variable. With increasing activity this may be so, but experience suggests that if activity decreases it is not so easy to reduce your labor costs.

At the beginning of this chapter, we stated that we make assumptions about cost behavior. It is your responsibility, as a manager, to determine to what extent these assumptions impair the analysis you are making.

Stepped and Mixed Costs

The assumptions we made about variable cost can also hold well with fixed costs, although in a short time period they are likely to stay the same. You will appreciate, however, that as activity increases a company may need to acquire more operating capability in the form of machinery and equipment. Our fixed costs will therefore increase to a higher level, and we will demonstrate this in the next section on break-even analysis.

Another factor is that some costs are a mix of fixed and variable. The cost for the supply of power, for example, may well consist of a standard charge for the delivery of the power and a variable cost representing the amount used. There are three methods that can be used to separate the total cost into the fixed and variable elements if that information is not readily available.

Account Analysis

This is a frequently used method and requires management to use its professional judgment and experience to determine the division of the total cost into its fixed and variable elements. For a manager with experience of the behavior of the costs incurred in production, reasonable estimates can be made.

Scattergraphs and Regression Analysis

Cost information from previous periods on a weekly or monthly basis and the division of the costs at various levels of activity can be identified.

High-Low Method

This is a popular method because it is a simple calculation and has an appealing logic. Once again, cost information from previous periods is used, and the costs and activity at the highest level and the lowest level during the period are identified. The following formula is then used:

$$\frac{\text{cost (highest level of activity – lowest level of activity)}}{\text{number of units (highest level of activity – lowest level of activity).}}$$

This formula is applied in Table 5.2.

Assuming that fixed costs stay the same, then the difference in the total costs of $375,000 must be due to variable costs and the increased activity of 375 additional units. The variable cost per unit must be $375,000 / 375 = $1,000. Proof is given by expanding Table 5.2 (see Table 5.3).

Break-Even Analysis

The assumption that fixed and variable costs behave differently in periods of fluctuating activity led to the development of break-even analysis. The question posed is "How many units do we have to produce and sell to break even, that is to make neither a profit nor a loss?" The following formula is used:

Table 5.2. High-Low Method

	Cost ($)	Number of units
Highest level of activity	600,000	450
Lowest level of activity	225,000	75
Difference	375,000	375

Table 5.3. High-Low Method Proof

	Number of units	Total variable cost (Units × VC per unit)	Total Cost ($)	Fixed cost = total cost – variable cost
Highest level of activity	450	$450,000	600,000	$150,000
Lowest level of activity	75	$75,000	225,000	$150,000

$$\$0 = SP(x) - VC(x) - TFC$$
$$SP = \text{selling price per unit}$$
$$VC = \text{variable cost per unit}$$
$$TFC = \text{total fixed cost}$$
$$x = \text{number of units.}$$

This relationship can be shown in the form of a break-even graph or chart. A basic example is shown in Figure 5.1. The activity levels are shown on the horizontal axis and the dollars on the vertical axis. The fixed costs will stay the same throughout the entire activity. Thus if the activity is 0, the fixed cost is the same as if the activity were 100%.

To the fixed costs, we add the variable costs to give the total cost line. The calculation is that at zero activity, the variable costs are zero, but the total costs will equal the fixed costs. As activity increases, the variable costs will increase in a linear relationship, and this is demonstrated by the total cost line.

Obviously, at zero activity the revenue is zero, and this is plotted as such. Once again we will assume that revenue increases in a linear

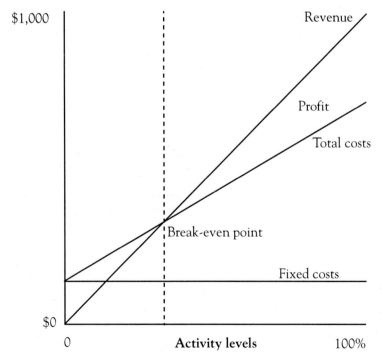

Figure 5.1. Break-even graph.

fashion. The point where the revenue line and the total cost line intersect is known as the break-even point. Above that point, we make a profit, and below that point we make a loss.

It is easy to identify the break-even point in Figure 5.1, in terms of both dollars and volumes. It is also possible to plot on the chart the margin of safety. This is the difference between the actual, or planned, level of activity and the break-even point. In other words, the margin of safety measures the amount by which the level of activity drops before the company arrives at its break-even point and then starts to make losses. The margin of safety can be measured in units of production or sales, sales value, or in percentage terms.

You will appreciate that in structuring Figure 5.1 we made some major simplifying assumptions about cost behavior. We have assumed that fixed and variable costs and even revenues will be perfectly linear over the full range of activity. This is highly unlikely, and the revenues and costs are likely to change.

Fixed costs are likely to demonstrate a stepped progression. As activity increases, at certain levels a company will have to expand its capacity. This may mean increasing the size of the factory or introducing more machinery or equipment. These additions will cause an increase in the fixed costs.

Variable costs are also likely to change over the full range of activity. It is not to do primarily with changes in price. Direct labor costs in the first few periods may be higher per unit because the workforce has a learning curve before they reach optimum efficiency. Material usage may also vary because of changes in production efficiency and wastage at different levels of activity. Finally, our revenue may change because we offer discounts at higher levels of production.

Because our simplifying assumptions are not valid over the complete range of activity, we can only make decisions and draw conclusions where the costs behave according to our assumptions. This range of activity where our assumptions hold up is known as the relevant range.

You most likely realized that as the revenue and variable cost per unit are assumed to be fixed, then the difference between the two amounts is also *fixed per unit* but will increase in *total* as activity increases. It is this important relationship that leads us to our next topic.

Cost Volume Profit Analysis

The break-even analysis shows us the level of activity where there is neither a profit nor a loss, but the underlying concepts can be used to expand this basic information. Cost Volume Profit (CVP) analysis uses the same basic assumptions that costs can be classified as either fixed or variable and that both costs and revenues are linear throughout the relevant range of activity. You may find in some countries this technique is referred to as "marginal costing."

If our price and variable cost per unit are assumed to remain the same, the difference between the two will remain the same but will increase or decrease in *total* as activity changes. This difference is known as the unit contribution margin and can be expressed as

$$CM = SP - VC,$$

where P is the selling price per unit and VC is the variable cost per unit. This is a powerful tool for assisting short-term decision making. Before we go any further, we can use basic data to demonstrate the usefulness of the contribution margin.

Where our revenue is $10 per unit and our variable costs per unit is $7, the contribution margin is $3. This is not a profit! It is a contribution toward the total fixed costs and, once those are recovered, the profit. If our fixed costs are $15,000 and our contribution margin is $3 per unit, our break-even point is $15,000 / $3 per unit = 5000 units. If we wish to make a profit of $6,000, then the total number of units we need to make and sell are as follows:

total fixed cost + target profit = $15,000 + $6,000 = $21,000 / $3 = 7,000 units.

Contribution margin can be thought of as the part of the selling price per unit that goes toward recovering the total fixed cost. Once the total fixed costs are recovered, in other words you reach break-even, the unit contribution margin is the amount each unit sale adds to profit. In some companies and countries, the term "contribution" may be used instead of contribution margin

As a manager, if you know the contribution margin of a product, you can easily calculate the break-even point and the profit or loss at different levels of activity. You can also quickly see how any increase or decrease in the revenue or variable cost per unit immediately impacts on the contribution margin and your break-even point.

For example, you may have a product with a selling price of $10 and the variable costs are $8. The contribution margin is then $2. In a financial period, the fixed costs are $30,000.

1. How many products do you need to sell to break even?

$$\$30,000 \ / \ \$2 = 15,000 \text{ units.}$$

2. You can increase the selling price to $11 and thus increase the contribution margin to $3. The break-even point is now

$$\$30,000 \ / \ \$3 = 10,000 \text{ units.}$$

3. You can reduce the variable costs to $6 per unit by investing in more machinery, thus increasing your fixed costs to $42,000 in a financial period.

New contribution margin = $4 per unit, so break-even point =
$$\$42,000 \ / \ \$4 = 10,500 \text{ units.}$$

These are only simple examples, but they illustrate the flexibility of the technique. Once it is established that variable costs stay the same per unit, several types of decisions can be explored. But remember that we are using a short-term decision-making technique.

We used a production example to explain the concept of contribution margin, but it is also valuable in a wider range of activities, including measuring efficiency in the operating room of a hospital.[2] It is argued that a surgical suite can schedule itself efficiently but fail to have a positive contribution margin. Some possible reasons for this are that surgeons are slow in the operations, and too many instruments or expensive implants are used. Variable costs, such as implants, vary directly with the volume of cases performed. The contribution margin per hour of operating room time is the hospital revenue generated by a surgical case, less all the hospitalization variable labor and supply costs.

A further step in our analysis is to calculate the contribution margin ratio. This is the percentage of contribution margin divided by the selling price per unit.

$$CMR = \frac{SP - VC}{SP} = \frac{CM}{SP}$$

CMR = contribution margin per unit
SP = selling price per unit
VC = variable cost per unit
CM = contribution margin per unit

The important principle in the application of this technique is that the contribution margin ratio will be the same for one unit as for the total production. This means that it can be used to ascertain the amount of sales dollars needed to earn a specific amount of profit by using the following formula:

$$\text{total sales in dollars} = \frac{\text{target profit + total fixed costs}}{\text{contribution margin ratio.}}$$

The following example shows the calculation of the contribution margin ratio for one unit and the calculation of the sales dollars needed for a certain amount of profit.

Example

A company has a product with a selling price of $10 and variable costs of $6. In the financial period, its fixed costs are expected to be $160,000, and it has budgeted for a profit of $40,000.

contribution margin ratio = SP − VC = $10 − $6 = $4 = 40%, or 0.4

sales in dollars = TP + TFC = $200,000 Divide $200,000 by the CM of 0.4 = total sales required of $500,000 or 50,000 units at $10 each

Proof

sales	50,000 units at $10 each	$500,000
Deduct		
variable costs 50,000 units at $6 each		$300,000
fixed costs		$160,000
Target profit		$40,000

Multiple Product Analysis

So far in this chapter, we have assumed that there is only one product. In reality, there are likely to be several products. The question is how do we apply the concepts of break-even and contribution margin in such a situation? If a company has a range of products that are basically similar, and the differentiation is only through color, flavor, or model type, the weighted average contribution margin can be used as in the following example.

Example

Twobuys Inc. produces a similar product with two model types: the Traditional and the Deluxe. Three Traditional models are sold for every one Deluxe. The budgeted fixed costs for the financial period are $200,000, and the per-unit figures are shown in Table 5.4.

To break even, the company would have to sell the following number of units:

$$\text{BEP in units} = \frac{\text{total fixed costs}}{\text{weighted average CM}} = \frac{\$200,000}{\$12.50.} = 16,000 \text{ units}$$

The total of 16,000 units would comprise the ratio of 3:1 units, so the Traditional would sell 12,000 units and the Deluxe for 4,000 units. These calculations are shown in Table 5.5.

You may note that in this example we did not allocate the fixed costs to the two different models but deducted them from the total contribution. We see the application of this approach again later in the chapter.

Table 5.4. Per-Unit Figures

	Traditional model ($)	Deluxe model ($)
Selling price	45	60
Variable costs	35	40
Contribution margin	10	20

$$\text{Weighted average contribution margin} = \frac{3(\$10) + 1(\$20)}{4} = \$12.50 \text{ per unit}$$

Table 5.5. Calculation of Break-Even Point

Proof	Traditional	Deluxe	Total
Number of units	12,000	4,000	16,000
Sales ($)	540,000	240,000	780,000
Variable costs ($)	420,000	160,000	580,000
Contribution margin ($)	120,000	80,000	200,000
Less fixed costs ($)			$200,000

Limitations of the Assumptions

We emphasized the limitations of our assumptions, but that does not mean you should downplay the concepts of break-even and contribution margin. As we see later in this chapter, it is extremely valuable for assisting in making a range of decisions; you just need to be aware of the limitations:

Fixed Costs

In practice, fixed costs will not stay at the same level throughout the full range of activity. As activity increases, a stage is reached where a company must invest in additional resources. This will introduce an incremental element of fixed cost and the stepped fixed-cost line we explained before.

Variable Costs

Variable costs are unlikely to stay the same per unit throughout the full range of activity. In the early stages, labor costs per unit may be higher while productivity is low, as the employees go through a learning curve. We then enter the relevant range where the variable costs are linear, but they may increase per unit at the upper end of activity due to overtime payments or excess wastage from human error. Similarly, direct material costs per unit may fluctuate but decrease as activity increases, as volume discounts and other reductions may be possible.

Discretionary Costs

There are some costs, such as advertising, research, and training, that may be discretionary. Managers may decide to increase or decrease such costs irrespective of activity levels.

Activity Levels

There may be more than one method for measuring activity. We have used the general term "a unit of production," but in some industries such identification may not be so easy. For example, in the transport industry, fuel costs will be influenced by the distance to be travelled and the weight of the load to be transported. In such cases, a hybrid unit may be required.

Inventory

We assume that the amount sold exactly equals the amount produced, and there is no inventory. If a company maintains low or constant inventory levels, then there is no problem, but you must be cautious in your analysis if there are significant changes in inventory levels during the financial period.

Variable Costing

Variable costing is a term that is used loosely to refer to the concept of what can be deemed as either a contribution margin statement or a variable cost statement. In other words, variable costing is a financial statement that concentrates on variable costs and ignores fixed costs. This approach changes your production cost and the cost of inventory. In this section, we use the term variable costing exclusively to the construction of a financial statement that emphasizes the contribution.

In chapter 4, when we looked at budgets, we observed that the purpose of a flexible budget was to capture the changes in activity levels and, hence, changes in variable costs. Our financial statements do the same, but there is a substantial impact on profit due to the treatment of fixed costs.

In Table 5.6, we show the production cost per unit figure using both full costing and variable costing for a company that produced 5,500 units in the financial period and sold 5,000 at $50.00 per unit, with the remaining 500 units going into the inventory at the end of the period. Using full costing, the fixed overhead of $16,500 has been charged to the cost unit on the basis of the number of units produced. Under both costing systems, the selling price is $50.00 per unit, but you can see that $1,500 of costs is transferred to inventory at the end of the period. Under variable costing, the full $16,500 of fixed costs will be charged against the sales figure as shown in Table 5.7.

The significance of the difference in costing methods on inventory valuation and profits is not important in many companies, as inventories

Table 5.6. Treatment of Inventory Costs

Full costing	Cost per unit ($)
Direct costs	30.00
Variable overhead	10.00
Fixed overhead (16,500 / 5,500)	3.00
Total full cost per unit	43.00
Value of closing inventory is 500 units at $43.00 per unit = $21,500.	
Variable costing	**Cost per unit ($)**
Direct costs	30.00
Variable overhead	10.00
Total variable cost per unit	40.00
Value of closing inventory is 500 units at $40.00 per unit = $20,000.	

Table 5.7. Inventory Costs and Impact on Profit

	Full costing ($)	Variable costing ($)
Sales (5,000 at $50)	**250,000**	**250,000**
Production cost of goods made (5,500)		
Direct costs	165,000	165,000
Variable overhead	55,000	55,000
Fixed costs	16,500	16,500
Total cost of production	236,500	236,500
Less closing inventory (500 units)	21,500	20,000
Cost of goods sold	**215,000**	**216,500**
Profit	35,000	33,500

are maintained at a low and consistent level. It should also be noted that for financial accounting and reporting purposes, companies are required to use full costing. However, it is important that you should realize the distinction in case you encounter it:

- If the units produced are equal in number to the units produced, there is no difference in profit.
- If the units produced are higher than the units sold, full costing will give a higher profit.
- If the units produced are lower than the units sold, variable costing will give a higher profit.

Dropping a Product Line

A major strategic decision made by any company is whether to drop a product line or to close a division or a factory. Many factors need to be taken into account, but there is the danger that the decision will be based on a full costing statement. For our demonstration, we will repeat the Twobuys Inc. example. However, we will make a slight change and delete the contribution margin line, as well as allocate the total fixed costs of $200,000 on the basis of the 16,000 units sold at a cost per unit of $12.50. The revised statement is shown in Table 5.8.

At this stage in the chapter, you can immediately analyze the issues. In a more complex situation, and with managers with little or no financial knowledge, there will be suggestions that the Traditional model is discontinued because it is making a "loss."

There are questions to ask in these situations:

Table 5.8. Revised Statement

	Traditional	Deluxe	Total
Number of units	12,000	4,000	16,000
Sales ($)	**540,000**	**240,000**	**780,000**
Variable costs ($)	420,000	160,000	580,000
Fixed costs ($)	150,000	50,000	200,000
Total costs ($)	**570,000**	**210,000**	**780,000**
Profit/(loss) ($)	(30,000)	30,000	780,000

1. Are the fixed overheads being allocated on a reasonable basis?
2. If we discontinue any one of the models, will this lead to a reduction in fixed overheads?
3. Is the model making a contribution to overheads?

The allocation of fixed overheads may not be on a reasonable basis, but the issue is whether we reduce fixed costs by dropping the Traditional model and whether this model is making a contribution. In the absence of other information, we assume that there is no reduction in fixed costs, and as the Traditional model is making a significant contribution of $120,000 toward them, it should be retained.

Probably the last question of the three gives us a golden rule: **If a product, division, department, or factory is making a contribution to fixed overheads, it should not be discontinued unless there are other reasons to justify discontinuation.**

Pricing Special Orders

Frequently managers are confronted with the possibility of winning a large order but only if a reduction in the normal selling price can be negotiated. Obviously, the manager needs to consider the impact on other customers, the possibility of this "special deal" being repeated, and the larger strategic direction of the company. To assist in the decision, the application of the contribution margin can be very useful. We use the example from the last section but restrict our discussions to the Traditional model (see Table 5.9).

If you are the manager of this model, and you are approached by a customer who offers to purchase 1,000 units of the model but at $40 a unit instead of the usual price of $45, you could do a mass of calculations,

Table 5.9. Traditional

Number of units	12,000
Sales ($)	**540,000**
Variable costs ($)	420,000
Fixed costs ($)	150,000
Total costs ($)	**570,000**
Profit/(loss) ($)	(30,000)

but the first question to ask is "Will it still make a contribution margin?" As the variable costs are $35 per unit, a contribution margin of $5 × 1,000 units will be made. Strictly on the cost analysis, this order would be worthwhile.

However, there is a slight twist. If the company continues to allocate the fixed costs on the basis of units sold, then the fixed costs will also increase, which seems ironic. This is not an argument against using full costing but advice to examine the decision you are making and what cost information you require.

Of course, there are other issues raised by accepting this special order. There is the danger that the customer wants all their orders to be at this price. There is also the problem if other customers want the same deal. You must also consider whether you have the spare capacity to accept the order. If, by accepting it, you have to reject an order at the higher price or invest in greater capacity (fixed costs), it would not be worthwhile.

The golden rule is this: **Assuming other things are equal, if an activity makes a contribution to fixed overheads, it is a worthwhile undertaking.**

Selecting the Most Profitable Alternative

Usually a company will have a range of products and may wish to concentrate its attention on the product that makes the most "profit." Once again, the contribution margin can be used to rank the products that produce the greatest benefits.

We can use the details from the example of Twobuys Inc. that had two models of their product with the unit selling price and costs shown in Table 5.10.

Given the choice of receiving either $10 or $20 contribution margin to fixed costs, it is safe to say that you would choose the latter. Assuming

Table 5.10. Selecting the Most Profitable Alternative

	Traditional model ($)	Deluxe model ($)
Selling price	45	60
Variable costs	35	40
Contribution margin	10	20

it is just as easy to sell the Deluxe model as it is to sell the Traditional model, and there are no significant factors, the general rule for ranking products is to concentrate on making the product that gives the highest contribution margin first, in order to cover the fixed costs the fastest and start making the business a profit as quickly as possible. The fixed costs do not need to be considered in this decision because they remain unchanged by the choice of model produced.

The disadvantage of ranking products according to the contribution per unit is that we ignore the market. If 10,000 units of the Traditional model and 4,000 units of the Deluxe model can be sold in 1 month, the total contribution margin for each product will be as follows:

$$\text{total contribution margin} =$$
$$\text{contribution margin per unit} \times \text{number of units sold.}$$

The ranking by total contribution would encourage you to revise your decision based on looking at the contribution per unit. If the predicted sales are valid, then it makes more financial sense to rank on the basis of the total contribution margin.

The golden rules for this are as follows:

- **If the number sold is not material to your decision, select the alternative that gives the largest contribution per unit.**
- **If the number sold is material, select the alternative that gives you the largest total contribution margin.**

Resource Scarcity

In the previous sections, we assumed that a company keeps on growing its present business: There are no restrictions. That is not the case, as there is usually some scarcity of resource or other limiting factor, such as shortages of materials or labor, a restriction on the sales demand at a particular price, or the production capacity of machinery. Therefore,

Table 5.11. Sales Volumes and Contribution Margins

	Traditional model	Deluxe model
Total contribution margin	$10 × 10,000 = $100,000	$20 × 4,000 = $80,000

limiting factors are the last aspect we will consider in making decisions using contribution margin analysis.

Where a company experiences a limiting factor, whether it is a ceiling on sales growth or a shortage of materials, managers must ensure that the contribution margin per limiting factor is maximized. The formula that is used is

$$\text{contribution margin per limiting factor} = \frac{\text{contribution margin per unit}}{\text{limiting factor per unit}}$$

Using our example of Twobuys Inc. again, we assume that variable costs represent a limiting factor that could be direct materials or direct labor. Using our variable costs as the limiting factor, we divide our contribution margin per unit by the variable costs per unit. If we apply this calculation, we obtain the result shown in Table 5.12.

If the variable costs represented a limited resource, it is financially sensible to concentrate on the Deluxe model that gives a contribution margin of 50 cents per unit compared to 29 cents from the Traditional model. If we find that there is a restricted demand for the Deluxe model, once that demand is met, we would switch the limited resource to the production of the Traditional model.

The golden rule from this is **if there is a scarce resource, select the alternative that gives the largest contribution margin per dollar of scarce resource.**

Table 5.13 draws together the results of the three different methods we use for ranking products, starting with the basic approach and increasing in level of sophistication until we find a method that takes account of factors that may constrain profitability.

You may wonder which is the correct approach. It depends on the environment you are in and your strategy. However, the concepts of cost behavior and the application of the contribution margin should assist you in making effective short-term decisions. In this chapter, we have given

Table 5.12. Applying a Limiting Factor

	Traditional model	Deluxe model
Contribution margin per unit	$10 = $0.29	$20 = $0.50
Limiting factor per unit	$35	$40

Table 5.13. Comparison of the Three Methods

	Traditional model	Deluxe model
Contribution margin per unit ($)	10	20
Ranking	2	1
Total contribution margin ($)	100,000	80,000
Ranking	1	2
Contribution per $ of variable costs ($)	0.29	0.50
Ranking	2	2

you guidance as to the type of situations that may arise and how you apply the techniques. But contribution margin is not the only technique, and we finish this chapter with a technique that ignores the classification of fixed and variable costs.

Incremental Analysis

Known under various names, incremental analysis, or relevant costing, was at one stage termed differential analysis. The concept of relevant cost arises when you have to choose between two or more alternatives or options. In order to calculate which option gives us the best benefit, we have to consider two factors:

1. What is the *differential* cost for each option?
2. Will the cost incur in the *future*?

In relevant cost decision-making, we take into account relevant costs such as *opportunity costs*. Opportunity costs are the benefits foregone when we choose one alternative over another. For example, if you have to give up your job to go back to college, then the salary foregone is the opportunity cost of your decision to return to college.

When calculating relevant costs, we ignore irrelevant costs. Irrelevant costs include fixed costs that do not change in the future, as well as *sunk costs*. The latter are costs that have occurred in the past and, thus, are irrelevant as they cannot be changed. Sunk costs have no effect on future costs. However, there is a psychological tendency for decision makers to include sunk costs as relevant in an effort to "recover" sunk costs[3] or a tendency to accelerate commitments to sunk costs.[4] In this respect, managers and management accountants must take care to separate sunk costs from future differential costs.

All of these terms capture the essence of the technique that was explained by Adelmann[5] many years ago. He referred to "differential analysis" as a technique for abandoning the constraints of full costing but not an alternative to it. It also completely disregards the fixed-variable cost classification that we have used so far.

Differential analysis only includes costs, both fixed and variable, and revenues that change due to a certain decision or event. Adelmann argues that when making a decision, it is quite possible that not only variable costs but also fixed costs are affected. In this instance we are interested not only in variable costs but in all types of costs that may be affected by that particular decision. He considers that these costs are relevant to that particular decision in that specific situation. An example illustrates how the technique is employed.

Digby Inc. relies on a generator that has only 1 year of useful life remaining. The costs of maintenance of the generator over its remaining life would be $1,000 per month. The amount of depreciation to be written off in the final year is $10,000, which would still need to be accounted for even with a replacement. The costs of running the generator, including fuel and the service of a part-time operator, are $10 per hour, and the generator runs for 2,500 hours per year. If the generator is retained, there would be refurbishment costs of $6,500.

The company has concern over the reliability of the existing generator and has the opportunity to purchase a new generator for $18,000, which would have a useful life of 1 year. The costs of running the new generator would be $7 per hour, and it would run for the same period of time as the existing generator. The maintenance costs would be $500 per month.

The company can make the decision by drawing up a financial statement that compares all the costs of the two alternatives (see Table 5.14).

If you look at Table 5.14, you see that some of the costs are the same for the two alternatives. We can therefore recast the table to only consider those costs that differ (see Table 5.15).

In Table 5.15, we only include those costs that differ between the two alternatives and are therefore relevant to the decision. In practice we need only to record the actual differences between the costs but the original amounts have been shown for clarity. In a complicated decision with

Table 5.14. Total Costs of the Alternatives

	Existing generator ($)	New generator ($)
Depreciation	10,000	10,000
Cost of acquisition	—	18,000
Running costs	25,000	17,500
Maintenance costs	12,000	6,000
Insurance	600	400
Refurbishment costs	6,500	—
Total	54,100	51,900

Table 5.15. Incremental Costs of the Alternatives

	Existing generator ($)	New generator ($)	Differential cost ($)
Cost of acquisition	—	18,000	18,000
Running costs	25,000	17,500	(7,500)
Insurance	600	400	(200)
Maintenance costs	12,000	6,000	(6,000)
Refurbishment costs	6,500	—	(6,500)
Total	44,100	41,900	(2,200)

many items of cost and possibly revenue to be considered, the paring down of the number of items reduces the possibility of confusion. You will also note that there is no distinction between fixed and variable costs.

Choosing the new generator, on financial grounds, seems the best decision, as it is $2,200 cheaper. Of course, you may want to consider the costs of breakdowns or losses in efficiency even if it seems financially the best alternative.

In this example, we used the total amounts involved in the decision, but as with CVP analysis, you can make your decision based on unit costs. One dilemma that managers frequently face is whether they should make a part themselves or outsource it. This is also known as the "make or buy" decision. If only variable costs will be affected, you can use CVP analysis, but if fixed costs are also likely to be affected, a comparison of all the relevant costs is required.

Let us take the example of a company that manufactures insulation tape for domestic use. It supplies the tape to hardware retailers at $6 per meter. Its variable costs are $2 per meter. The company's current production output is 6,000 meters per month, and it is contemplating increasing that production by 50% per month. Fixed costs would not be affected.

The only change in the figures will be the 50% increase in revenue and variable costs. The contribution margin is $4 per meter, and an extra 3,000 meters will give an additional contribution margin of $12,000.

Upon further investigation, the company determines that the increased production will also increase fixed costs by $10,000 per month. Our analysis so far shows that the additional contribution margin covers the additional fixed costs to give a profit of $2,000. But as fixed costs will also change, we may wish to draw up a simple statement of all the relevant costs (see Table 5.16).

Not surprisingly, we arrive at the same conclusion using the two techniques. Managers sometimes wonder which is the best technique: CVP or incremental costing. Both of the techniques are concerned with identifying the relevant costs when making the decision. The relevant costs are those that change. In CVP analysis, the assumption is made that only variable costs will change, and fixed costs remain the same. In incremental costing, the assumption is that some fixed costs will change.

In making the decision, there are the questions you need to ask when selecting the appropriate technique:

1. What is the decision that needs to be made?
2. What are the alternatives?
3. What cost information do we have or can we obtain?
4. Can we classify the costs into fixed and variable components?
5. Will only the variable costs change?
6. Will some of the fixed costs change?

If you have the information, and only variable costs change, you can use CVP analysis. If fixed costs are also likely to change, use incremental

Table 5.16. Incremental Cost Statement

	$
Incremental sales (3,000 meters @ $6)	18,000
Incremental variable costs (3,000 meters @ $2)	(6,000)
Incremental fixed costs	(10,000)
Profit	2,000

costing. CVP analysis does have the advantage of being very flexible in its application. Incremental costing has the advantage of ensuring that all relevant costs, both fixed and variable, are taken into account.

Conclusions

In this chapter, we discussed a group of techniques designed to provide managers with tools to make decisions among different alternatives. The first part of the chapter concentrated on the classification of fixed and variable costs. This division was then used to explain how you calculate the break-even point. This technique allows you to answer the question "How many units do we have to produce and sell to break even, that is to make neither a profit nor a loss?"

We built on this analysis to discuss CVP, which is a powerful tool for assisting short-term decision making. It uses the same basic assumptions that costs can be classified as either fixed or variable and that both costs and revenues are linear throughout the relevant range of activity. This difference between the selling price and variable cost per unit is known as the contribution margin. It stays the same per unit but increases in total as activity increases.

We demonstrated how knowledge of contribution margin could be used to solve the following:

- Dropping a product line where the rule is if a product, division, department, or factory is making a contribution to fixed overheads, it should not be discontinued unless there are other reasons to justify discontinuation.
- Pricing a special order where the rule is, assuming other things are equal, if an activity makes a contribution to fixed overheads, it is a worthwhile undertaking.
- Selecting the most profitable alternative where the rules are such if the number of units sold is not material to your decision, select the alternative that gives the largest contribution per unit, but if the number of units that are sold is material, select the alternative that gives you the largest contribution margin.

- Dealing with a resource scarcity where the rule is that, if there is a scarce resource, select the alternative that gives the largest contribution margin per dollar of scarce resource.

One disadvantage with CVP analysis is it makes the assumption that a decision involves only changes in revenues and *variable* costs. However, in certain situations, it is quite possible that not only variable costs but also fixed costs will be affected. In this instance, we are interested not only in variable costs but in any costs that may be *relevant* to that particular decision, and this may include certain fixed costs.

Both CVP analysis and incremental costing are concerned with identifying the *relevant* costs when making the decision. The relevant costs are those that change. Relevant costs include opportunity costs and should be included. Sunk costs are irrelevant and should be excluded. In CVP analysis, the assumption is made that only variable costs change and fixed costs remain the same. In incremental costing, the assumption is that *some* fixed costs will change.

In selecting alternative strategies, part of the analysis will be based on a cost-benefit approach, but you should also recognize any nonfinancial characteristics that may be important from the strategic viewpoint. In other words, when using strategic cost analysis, you must broaden your horizon to incorporate considerations such as industry structure, market composition, ownership structure, demand and supply variables, interest rates, political changes, inflation or deflation, management compensation, regulatory changes, and globalization. Strategic cost analysis contributes toward the development of strategy and records progress toward its achievement; it does not replace strategy.

CHAPTER 6

Strategic Cost Management

About This Chapter

In this final chapter, we consider a number of techniques that have emerged over recent years. This moves us from the concentration on analysis to the broader view of management, although it would be difficult to draw the dividing line.

As we moved through the 20th century, the costing of manufacturing processes and the tangible assets associated with them shifted to knowledge-based assets and strategies to manage those intangible assets. Managerial thinking changed, and the practice of imposing systems and decisions from the top down without question developed into more participative styles.

These developments, and other changes, led to the rethinking of strategic formulation and the cost information required. The new business environment of organizational empowerment, competitive capabilities, and core competencies required the collection and reporting of cost and other data that are future-orientated and that recognize the external environment and the importance of nonfinancial as well as financial inputs.

In this chapter, we review the main techniques and their importance to you as a manager. Remember that the methods and techniques discussed in this and previous chapters are not substitutes for good management. They are there to inform, illuminate, and support management planning, control, and decision making.

Key Definition

Strategic cost management is the application of cost management techniques to simultaneously improve the strategic position of a firm and reduce costs.[1]

Both academic thinking and practitioners' experiences have developed and modified the methods and techniques we discuss in this chapter. One major line of thinking has been the work of Prahalad and Hamel,[2] and we commence the chapter with a brief review of their contribution. This is followed by an examination of two techniques that most managers will have heard of: value chain analysis and the balanced scorecard. This is followed by considering cost reduction, and in that section, we provide some very practical advice for the reduction of overhead costs. The latter half of the chapter examines different approaches to performance evaluation and improvement processes.

None of the topics discussed in this chapter are replacements or alternatives to the various methods and techniques we explained in earlier chapters. As you read through our explanations, you will appreciate that all the topics require reliable cost data for strategic purposes. Without this information, you could not implement them successfully in any organization.

Core Competencies

If we look for a conceptual framework that underpins many of the techniques explained in this chapter, then it is to be found in the works of Prahalad and Hamel on core competencies. They contended that, where companies have areas of significant competitive advantage, these can be used as the structure of the organization's overall strategy. If it is difficult for competitors to replicate these core competencies, they can be exploited to increase customer-perceived value.

Core competencies are the skills and technologies that have been developed throughout an organization. It is the aggregate of the learning processes by individuals and groups across the learning organization. In the next section where we consider the balanced scorecard, we can see how it embraces the acquisition, cultivation, and exploitation of core competencies in which an organization excels and gains a competitive advantage.

Hamel and Prahalad coined the term "strategic architecture" to explain the process by which an organization manages its core competencies to enjoy future competitive success. Strategic architecture can be considered as a roadmap or a plan that charts the way to the organization's future success. The plan is not concerned with improvements in present performance but with the nurturing of core competencies to provide strengths for enjoying future successes in emerging opportunities. It sets out not only where the organization is going but also the steps it must take to get there.

Although conceptually appealing, there are difficulties in how strategic architecture is to be applied at the specific organizational level, a criticism that the authors acknowledged. The core competencies must be capable of being recognized and articulated in such a way that they can be managed. Their presence needs to be communicated throughout the organization to contribute toward strategy development.

Strategic Positioning

Research conducted by Al-Hazmi[3] led him to conclude that "market instability stimulates strategic movement and cost information is being used in management thinking to support strategic development in meeting competitive pressures and in restructuring and reconfiguration of business strategy." In this section, we discuss two techniques that adopt a holistic view of the organization and look toward the future but with the benefit of knowledge from the past.

Value Chain Analysis

An organization may be very proficient at developing strategy, but it must also be able to implement it at every stage in the organization's operations. Value chain analysis is a technique that enables an organization to focus on each separate operation and to ensure that it adds value to the product or service. The value chain was developed by Porter,[4] but there have been additions, modifications, and other claimed improvements by consultants and academics over the years.

The first stage in the technique is to identify the process of value added that is performed in the industry of which the organization is a part. For example, an organization may have a value chain that looks like the diagram shown in Table 6.1.

This is only a simple layout, and in practice the value chain analysis would require much more detail, depending on the industry and the nature of the organization. The emphasis of the analysis is the

Table 6.1. Value Chain

Process	Value added by
Procurement of inputs costs	Suppliers
Research and design costs	Company
Capital costs	
Operating costs	
Administration costs	
Distribution costs	Distributor
After service costs	Company

examination of the entire chain of operations and the contribution made by the particular company.

When the diagram is complete, an analysis can be conducted of the entire value chain to determine the organization's current and potential competitive advantages. In conducting this analysis, the organization will be weighing up its core competencies and determining whether its strategic competitive advantage is cost leadership or differentiation.

The analysis will also seek to identify opportunities for adding value. This may be the introduction of computerized procedures, expanded services to customers, or use of just-in-time delivery of raw materials. The scrutiny of the value chain should also highlight potential areas of cost reduction, which may lead to decisions about outsourcing certain activities where the organization is not competitive.

An organization should be able to calculate the makeup of costs all the way from the raw materials phase to the end price paid by the ultimate customer on a value chain. Strategic cost analysis can be restricted not only to one's own internal costs but also to suppliers, distribution channels, and competitors. By including the impact of costs both inside and outside the company, the value chain helps the managers understand the total sum of the shifting costs throughout the chain. Strategies are then developed to address the ramifications of the costs.

The value chain is revealing but not simple to construct. Despite the complications of the task, the value chain gives benefits by exposing the cost competitiveness of your position and the potential strategic alternatives.

The Balanced Scorecard

The balanced scorecard provides a framework for managers to use by linking different performance measurements together. This tool assists managers to clarify their vision for the organization and translate their vision into measurable actions that employees can understand and enables managers to balance the concerns of various stakeholders. "The indicators should measure performance against the critical success factors of the business, and the 'balance' is the balancing tension between the traditional financial and nonfinancial operational, leading and lagging, and action-oriented and monitoring measures."[5]

The balance scorecard allows managers to focus on both financial and nonfinancial measures to assess performance. It translates an organization's vision, mission, and strategy into an integrated set of performance measures that can be evaluated in the form of a report card: the scorecard.

The concept is based on the proposition that there are four critical success factors (CSFs) or perspectives that encapsulate the strategy of the organization. For each of these factors, the organization needs to develop three to five measures.

- *Financial perspective.* This uses traditional financial measures such as return on investment to assess whether the organization is meeting its financial objectives.
- *Customer perspective.* By using such measures such as growth in market share, number of new customers, and customer satisfaction surveys, the organization seeks to ascertain whether the customers' expectations are being met.
- *Internal business process perspective.* This evaluates the effectiveness and efficiency of managing the internal operations or value chain: the organization's success in improving critical business processes. There are three areas of attention: innovation, operations, and postsales service.
- *Learning and growth perspective.* This assesses the organization's abilities in adapting, innovating, and growing. There are four factors that are measured: goal congruence (measured by satisfaction ratings), skill and process development (measured by the percentage of employees trained), workforce empowerment

(measured by the percentage of line workers making management decisions), and enhanced information system capabilities (measured by the percentage of processes with real-time feedback).

It is essential that there is a balance among the four dimensions, and one critical success factor should not predominate. There should also be a balance between quantitative and nonquantitative measures. They should be forward looking, as well as backward looking, and both short term and long term. The relationships among the four dimensions can be shown in the form of a diagram or strategy map. Some companies in the oil and chemical industries, such as Mobil Corporation, have come up with a fifth CSF for the balance scorecard: the environmental perspective.

Implementing a balance scorecard requires a substantial amount of work and is best carried out by a team of managers from different areas of the organization. The stages they would go through are as follows:

- *Stage 1: Preliminary evaluation.* This would involve evaluating the external environment and the organization and its strategy. It would also evaluate the financial position, human and capital resources, and the procedures and processes being used.
- *Stage 2: Implementation plan.* This would consist of meetings with managers to explain the project, discuss its objectives, and gain support.
- *Stage 3: Development of objectives, measures, and buy-in.* The goal is to achieve consensus on objectives and to establish a cause-and-effect linkage across objectives at both senior and midlevel management.
- *Stage 4: Measures and targets.* There should be a clear, unambiguous measure for each target so that managers know what they are expected to achieve.
- *Stage 5: Agreement.* Middle and senior managers should agree on the responsibilities for each area and on the objective and understand the method for measuring performance.
- *Stage 6: Top management support.* Top management should be involved throughout the process, but it is essential that they understand, agree, and sign off on the system.

There are difficulties in implementing and maintaining a balanced scorecard. By its implementation, we are contemplating significant organizational change, and there can often be strong resistance. Implementation can be time consuming and expensive. The measures and targets may be difficult to set and open to criticism at the time they are established or later when they are in operation. It is also a long process and it is frequently found that there is what may be termed "system innovation syndrome." This is where the team, as well as other managers, responsible for implementing the balanced scorecard becomes exhausted by the exercise. Short-cuts are taken, inappropriate and ambiguous measures and targets are set, and some managers retain the old methods.

There is also a tendency for the balanced scorecard to be regarded as a "macho management trophy." At executive meetings, figures may be traded as if they are blood pressure measures. The true value of the balanced scorecard will only be appreciated if the implementation is robust and rigorous, and the same meticulous thought is given to keeping it updated. Lewy and Du Mee (1998) have come up with the "10 commandments" of do's and don'ts when developing an effective balance scorecard.[6]

Cost Reduction

According to Brierly, Cowton, and Drury, "A cost can be a vague and indeterminate concept, and as a consequence a variety of costs can be identified for reduction."[7] To assist you in identifying what the costs are and how and why you should reduce them, we explain various methods such as target costing, life-cycle costing, and activity-based management in this section.

Before we look at these, we look at some very practical general advice on cost reduction given in the *Harvard Business Review*.[8] The advice proposed ways to reduce overheads by 10%, 20%, and 30%. We briefly comment on a few of these suggestions for the 10% level:

- Although discretionary perks and activities can be cut out,
  if too savage it may reduce employee morale. However, such
  activities may be consolidated for cost savings. For example,

some events may be turned into multidepartmental, thus allowing some of the costs to be shared.

- Assess the amount of supervisory management required. If the work is repetitive and has little change-over time, reduced supervision may be possible.
- Analyze expenditures on miscellaneous items such as telephone calls, stationery, technology add-ons, and travel and entertaining expenses.

As the authors of the article point out, many of the cost reductions they suggest at the 10% level can be made without disrupting the interactions with other departments. These are not strategic applications to cost reduction but are offered as an encouragement for you to consider all activities for which you are responsible. Having looked at the practical advice, we will now consider more complex techniques. It may be that you are not in a management position to implement these, but a knowledge of the concepts will enhance your knowledge of the issues and also explain some of the actions taken by senior management or midlevel managers in other departments.

Target Costing

Traditionally, companies price their products or services using the cost-plus model, and some still do. Essentially, this uses the average costs (variable and fixed) to which a mark-up is added in the form of a percentage to give the market price. This approach is only feasible if the market is noncompetitive or only slightly competitive.

The danger of the cost-plus model is that changes may have occurred in the market environment where the organization has traditionally operated. Prospective customers now have access to the Internet to trace alternative sources of supply, which may be cheaper or of better quality. Products often have a shorter life than previously, so the pricing must be right to gain the maximum advantage in the shortest time. There is also the problem of competition from companies choosing cost leadership as a strategy.

To remedy the deficiencies of the cost-plus model, organizations turn to target costing, which is often referred to as price-led costing. The market decides the price, and cost containment is essential. Target costing was developed by Toyota in Japan during the 1960s.[9] This technique ensures that the product is introduced to the market with a specific functionality, quality, and selling price. It is also planned that the product can be produced at a life-cycle cost that generates an acceptable level of profitability.[10]

Key Definition

Target costing involves the establishment of target costs for each product and each product-related activity, starting with the design of the product and culminating with the sale of the product.[11] Thus this process requires information relating to the organization's competitive product and supply chain strategies. Target costing is a reversal of the cost-plus model, and we start with the market price. The organization uses market research information to determine the price customers are willing to pay given the product's functionality and quality and the alternatives provided by competitors. We then deduct the profit we wish to make, and the balance is the target cost we must achieve to be successful. The target cost is the maximum cost that is allowable in the production, distribution, and disposal of the product:

$$\text{target cost} = \text{target selling price} - \text{target profit}.$$

It is essential that an organization examine all the product costs in the product cycle and not focus on a narrow range. A balance must also be maintained, and an organization must be careful that the cost reductions achieved in one area are outweighed by the cost increases suffered by another area as a consequence. Integration of effort can be enhanced by using a team approach.

One area that is frequently not investigated is that of design. Comparatively small changes in design can lead to considerable reductions in production costs. Value engineering is performed to redesign the product and *kaizen* costing (also known as continuous improvement) is performed to streamline its manufacturing and distribution processes. It is essential that designers and production managers share their expertise in order to achieve the target cost.

In implementing target costing, it is valuable that you have a good grasp of the relationship of the components of fixed and variable costs and of how they behave both long term and short term. It may be that by increasing fixed costs, such as by greater mechanization, variable costs in the form of labor can be reduced. Variable or fixed costs may also be reduced by outsourcing, but this is a decision that should not be taken lightly.

Target costing is not a complex technique, but it is essential that the entire process is analyzed as follows:

- Calculate the target cost that satisfies the market price and the organization's target profit.
- Evaluate the types of actions that may be implemented in different departments or areas to bring actual costs in line with the target.
- Assess whether the reduction in costs in one area may lead to a consequential increase in costs in other areas.
- Set targets for each area in discussion with managers.
- Monitor the cost reductions to ensure that the actions implemented produce the required results.

Life-Cycle Costing

On a personal basis, you will most likely be familiar with the concept of life-cycle costing. If you are considering buying a new car, you will not only consider the cost of the car. If you are financing the purchase, then you will have to pay interest over several years. There is also the question of insurance and maintenance and repairs. Some models of cars are renowned for being expensive for parts! Finally, you will want to know how the car holds its value and what it may be worth when you come to exchange it.

Companies are increasingly concerned with the life-cycle cost when they either purchase an item or manufacture it. For example, if a company is implementing a new computerized system, there is not only the initial cost of purchasing it. There will be the training costs of staff to operate the system and the possible costs of the supplier for maintenance, breakdowns, and upgrades. There is also likely to be the less quantifiable costs of the disruption caused during the implementation period. There may even be costs associated with running the old system and the new system until there is confidence in its efficiency.

There have been four categories of life-cycle costs proposed. These are research and development cost, production and construction cost, operation and maintenance support cost, and retirement and disposal cost. The importance of each component will vary from company to company and over time.

Retirement and disposal costs have become increasingly important as environmental legislation compels companies to remedy damage that is caused by their operations. Product design costs at one time were not carefully controlled, but it is now apparent that the nature of design will to a large extent determine the production costs. Careful design with an understanding of the production processes can reduce costs substantially.

There is an added complication with some of these costs, as they will be incurred at some future date. This introduces the concept of the time value of money. If asked whether you would prefer to spend $10,000 now or in 20 years' time, you would pick the former. This is not only because of inflation, but if you have $10,000 now and invest it, even at a low interest rate, it will become substantially more than $10,000. Working backwards, the $10,000 in 20 years' time is worth less now. This means that future cash flows need to be discounted to their present value.

Life-cycle costing has several advantages. It is future oriented, and it compels managers to examine the long-term financial implications of the strategic decisions they are making. It also encourages managers to examine and question the costs incurred at every significant stage in the life of the product. The purposes for which organizations could choose to use life-cycle costing are the acquisition of a system or project on long-term budgets and operating results and the comparison among competing suppliers of products and services. Repair costs, maintenance, and warranties are all other concerns that encourage management to look at the life-cycle costing.[12]

Unfortunately, there is a tendency for deep analysis when the decision is being made but for very little monitoring and control afterwards. Although managers carefully predict the costs to be incurred over the life of the asset, few ensure that actual costs are compatible with predictions. This lack of control and monitoring may be because the accounting records, once the decision is made, consolidate the costs of maintenance and similar expenditures under one heading for the entire department or organization.

Activity-Based Management (ABM)

This term has become increasingly used, at least in textbooks, and some managers would argue that they have always practiced ABM but merely regarded it as good management. Having said that, the technique formalizes practices, is a logical extension of activity-based costing (ABC), and reflects the concepts of value chain analysis but give them a narrower focus.

Unlike the traditional cost approach, ABM regards the organization as a set of interlinked processes that create and deliver value to customers. The most basic concept in ABM is that of an "activity," hence its relationship with ABC. As explained in an earlier chapter, ABC identifies the relationship between overhead costs and activities. It uses the concepts of cost pools that capture the overhead costs of specific activities and that specify cost drivers. These drivers cause the costs of those activities that we analyze to determine an allocation rate. ABM extends this by taking the information computed by ABC and analyzing the activities to reduce costs.

There are two main aspects to the application of ABM. One is ascertaining those activities that do not add value and eliminating or reducing them. Activities are non-value-adding if their elimination would not affect the customer's perceived value of the product or service or impair the functioning and operation of the organization.[13,14,15] You will appreciate the relationship between this aspect and value chain analysis. The second aspect is to ascertain which activities add value so that we can enhance them. ABM will also seek to improve the efficiency and effectiveness of all major activities and identify new value-added activities.

If we consider typical non-value-added activities in a manufacturing environment, the following are the obvious ones:

- *Storage and internal transport of raw materials, work in process, and finished goods.* These can be significant and may be reduced by using systems such as just-in-time deliveries of supplies and configuring the production lines to reduce movements of work in process and finished goods.

- *Idle time and down time.* It may be more financially beneficial to conduct regular maintenance and employ progress chasers to ensure that capacity is functioning at its most efficient.

These examples are from a manufacturing environment, but you can apply the principles to any type of activity. A key factor to concentrate on is the wastage of time. This is costly, and often means that the customer is also waiting. In some service industries, customers may regard waiting as a normal part of the activity, but speedy service is usually expected.

If you are a manager in a company where ABC is successfully implemented, you should have no difficulties in adopting ABM. Even if your company has a poor costing system, the concepts of eliminating or reducing non-value-added activities and enhancing value-added activities can still be applied.

Performance Evaluation and Improvement

We made the point in an earlier chapter that you get what you measure. Evaluation of performance will depend on the measure you are using for the performance. If it is not well crafted, the performance measure may have been achieved but not the underlying strategic objective.

The desirable characteristics of performance measures, whether for groups or individuals are that they

- are credible and understandable,
- measure the performance desired,
- do not conflict with other measures in the organization,
- are aligned to the organizational strategic objectives,
- reflect the responsibilities of the employee or group,
- are capable of change where necessary.

Even with great care, performance measures may not reflect all these characteristics. In attempting to capture the essence of activities, it is possible to derive a measure that is too complex to be understood by the employee. It may also be that the measure does not take account of events outside the employee's control. Sometimes decisions that affect your own performance will be made at a higher level or outside of the organization, such as a change in regulations.

Strategic Business Units

A strategic business unit (SBU) consists of clearly defined operating activities that are controllable by the SBU manager. In essence, the concept of an SBU mirrors some of the arguments of "beyond budgeting" that we discussed in chapter 5. The manager of an SBU normally has autonomy for decision making and monitoring and controlling all aspects of the resources of the SBU. It is the notion of "controllability" of costs that makes the SBU system fair and that acts as an incentive for managers.

Usually there will be an agreement or contract with the manager setting out the responsibilities, the measurable performance required, and the incentive for doing so. The incentive should be set at such a level that the manager is highly motivated to achieve the performance measures. In establishing SBUs, an organization chooses to be decentralized, where local mangers of SBUs have considerable responsibility in planning, control, and decision making, as opposed to a centralized organization, where top-level management controls the various subunits.

The types of SBUs are similar to the responsibility centers we discussed earlier, except the degree of managerial autonomy is much higher in SBUs. The following are the main types you will encounter:

- *Cost SBUs.* These do not generate revenues or profits but provide a product or service at an agreed cost. Examples are maintenance SBUs, dispatching SBUs, and information technology SBUs.
- *Revenue SBUs.* These are concerned solely with generating revenue and do not have responsibility for costs.
- *Profit SBUs.* They have the responsibility for both revenues and costs. They are expected to generate a predetermined level of profit.
- *Investment SBUs.* They have responsibility for the investment in assets that generate the profit.

A variety of measures can be used to evaluate the performance of the SBUs. These may be simple financial measures, such as achievement of budgeted costs or profits, or can be more sophisticated and use financial ratios such as profit margins and return on investment. Sometimes nonfinancial measures may be used in addition to give comprehensive measures of performance, and these may be incorporated in a balanced scorecard for the SBU.

Even with well-established and agreed performance measures and a robust incentive scheme, it is possible managers will find ways to massage the performance measures to achieve the reward. In particular, they may have a short-term focus or attempt to shift costs.

Managers will usually receive their incentive in the form of a bonus based on annual measures. They are, therefore, motivated to concentrate on performance in the short term rather than to plan for the long term. Costs that should be spent on maintenance, employee training, new products, or process initiatives and similar long-term investments are ignored. This becomes an even greater issue when an SBU manager anticipates rapid promotion if the performance measures are met. It will be left to the successor to address the problems.

Cost shifting can take different forms and may be due to managers purposely shifting some costs outside of their responsibility, or where there is ambiguity in the range of their responsibilities, ignoring some of the consequences of their actions.

We have already discussed the issue of managers and uncontrollable costs, and this is an area where a manager may shift costs. If we consider a cost SBU, it would seem only fair that a manager should be responsible for only those costs that can be controlled. In the majority of instances, these will be variable costs, and the manager will not be responsible for fixed costs. A manager may therefore take action to shift costs from the variable definition to the fixed definition.

There are also situations where, for the benefit of their own SBU, managers may make a decision that has an adverse effect on SBUs elsewhere in the organization or even outside the organization. It could be argued that the just-in-time system shifts the costs of holding raw materials partly to the supplier and partly to society in the form of pollution and crowded roads at inconvenient times.

Cost Allocation

The measures used to evaluate the performance of managers in discharging their responsibilities will include an element of indirect costs or overheads that may be significant. As we saw in our explanation of full costing, the allocation of central overheads is arbitrary. Managers may find that they have the responsibility of overheads that they are unable to control. Unfortunately, they may take actions that enhance their performance measures but are detrimental to the monitoring and control of the entire organization.

Several of the indirect costs such as electricity, rent, cleaning, and refurbishments may be allocated on the space occupied by a department. A devious manager may attempt to reduce the space that his or her department occupies, thus reducing the amount of overhead allocated to the department. The manager may feel virtuous because the amount of overhead has been reduced, which reflects more favorable performance measures. However, the organization still has that space and the overheads. Organizationally, there are no benefits.

Cost allocation is also a major issue with SBUs. Where there are central costs such as IT, maintenance, and human resources being provided centrally and the costs allocated, there may be an incentive for the manager to use outside sources if they are less expensive or offer other benefits. The use and charge for central services is frequently a controversial area where there are no immediate solutions.

Total Quality Management (TQM)

Strategic cost analysis is used to improve organizational performance, whether this is in a hospital, bank, manufacturer, restaurant, or any other type of organization. The size and nature of the organization will determine the cost data it requires. But the purpose of the analysis is to seek improvements in performance. In this last section, we discuss total quality management

You will find that parts of our explanation repeat and build upon the advice we gave in earlier chapters on measuring and monitoring performance; some parts echo the principles and practices of value chain analysis and balanced scorecards. Other parts capture the notions of cost cutting and cost reduction.

The philosophy and practice of TQM encapsulates all aspects of an organization so that every business discipline and profession can call it their own. Whether you are in accounting, marketing, production, or any other functions, you will be involved in TQM if your organization decides to implement it.

But be careful: Quality has multiple meanings. Customers can perceive quality as

- luxury compared to other products or services, even if you have to wait for it;
- delivery at the time promised and the price agreed;
- consistency, in that the product or service is exactly the same no matter at which outlet you purchase it or at what time;
- the availability of spare parts or quick service time.

The first stage in implementing TQM is to analyze your customer expectations and to develop measures to capture them. These can be both quantitative, such the time taken for a repair to be conducted, or nonquantitative, such as the enhancement to personal image that the customer hopes to achieve by buying the product or servise.

Fortunately, there is considerable agreement on the principles and practices of TQM. Although different sources emphasize various components, a list of the 12 factors that most agree on has been constructed:[16]

1. *Committed leadership.* A near-evangelical, unwavering, long-term commitment by top managers to the philosophy, usually under a name something like Total Quality Management, Continuous Improvement (CI), or Quality Improvement (QI).
2. *Adoption and communication of TQM.* Using tools like the mission statement and themes or slogans.
3. *Closer customer relationships.* Determining customers' (both inside and outside the firm) requirements, then meeting those requirements no matter what it takes.
4. *Closer supplier relationships.* Working closely and cooperatively with suppliers and ensuring they provide inputs that conform to customers' end-use requirements.

5. *Benchmarking.* Researching and observing the best competitive practices.

6. *Increased training.* Usually includes TQM principles, team skills, and problem solving.

7. *Open organization.* Lean staff, empowered work teams, open horizontal communications, and a relaxation of traditional hierarchy.

8. *Employee empowerment.* Increased employee involvement in design and planning, and greater autonomy in decision-making.

9. *Zero-defects mentality.* A system in place to spot defects as they occur, rather than through inspection and rework.

10. *Flexible manufacturing.* Applicable only to manufacturers. Can include just-in-time inventory, cellular manufacturing, design for manufacturability (DFM), statistical process control (SPC), and design of experiments (DQE).

11. *Process improvement.* Reduced waste and cycle times in all areas through cross-departmental process analysis.

12. *Measurement.* Goal orientation and zeal for data, with constant performance measurement, often using statistical methods.

We are able, therefore, to describe TQM in general terms and also to indicate the particular role of strategic cost accounting. The main cornerstones of TQM are customer satisfaction and continuous quality improvement in all processes and functional areas of the organization, including research and design, production, marketing, finance, and information systems.

You need to consider who the customers are. The immediate buyer may not be the final user of the product or service. Suppliers, insofar as they have business relationships with the organization, can be considered as having the same needs as customers insofar as ethical trading and clarity on the organization's needs when purchasing. Some would argue that there are even internal customers, such as employees who are frequently completing their work to satisfy the next stage in the production process.

Continuous improvement assumes that all processes, procedures, and practices can be improved. Frequently, the best suggestions for improvements are generated by the employees doing the specific job. TQM encourages employee empowerment, but at the same time, the essential integration of processes and procedures must be obtained. The use of multidepartmental teams can minimize possibilities of disruptions through partial implementation of improvements.

There are many claimed benefits of TQM. Companies that implemented it not only speak of the time and cost in doing so but also express pleasure with the visible improvements that are introduced. The gains that organizations have made include

- a reputation as a quality organization;
- reduction in costs without lowering of quality and often with quality being improved;
- increases in financial measures such as profit margins and return on investment;
- the ability to charge higher prices for products and services than previously;
- better customer-retention levels and a decrease in returned goods and repairs under guarantees;
- an increase in presence in new markets both nationally and internationally;
- better working relationships with suppliers, sometimes leading to reduced purchasing costs and better delivery times;
- speedier response times to changes in the market and customer preferences.

Organizations have found problems in introducing TQM and have abandoned it or decided on partial implementations. The difficult issues have been the following:

- Agreeing which customers they are trying to satisfy and how those customers perceive quality. There may be a customer chain, and if the final customer is not satisfied, the displeasure may result in a lowering of sales or in other customers in the chain seeking alternative suppliers.
- Identifying appropriate measures of quality and being regularly able to collect, analyze, and feed back this data to employees.
- Attempting to achieve employee empowerment but at the same time ensuring integration of all the processes and functions.

- Seeking continuous improvements but also attempting to benefit from the gains of consistency and from standardization of procedures and practices.

The final question is whether TQM is for you and your organization. In a very well-constructed study in the United States, the value of TQM was assessed. As with all academic studies, the researchers pointed out that there were limitations to their research but concluded, "The message for managers is that, although TQM programs can produce performance advantages, they do not address the needs of all organizations, and they are fraught with pitfalls for firms that lack the requisite complementary resources."[17] Although this article is dated 1995, we believe that the words of caution are as valid now as they were then.

The Final View

In reading this book, you may have realized that, in the early chapters, we identify what we mean by cost, and in the final chapter, we expound on the strategic management of cost. The early chapters provide the foundations of strategic cost analysis, and the later chapters explain more advanced techniques.

You are not able to apply the techniques in chapters 5 and 6 unless you thoroughly understand the content of the preceding chapters. You must also remember that the techniques are mostly described in the form of theoretical models. What takes place in your own organization may have a more practical approach. You need to reread chapter 1 so that you can identify the influences on your own strategic cost analysis.

In summary, the conceptual ordering of the chapters has been as follows.

Chapters 1 and 2

- How do we identify cost in different types of organization and how might they impact strategy?
  - Classification of cost
  - Absorption costing
  - Activity-based costing
  - Time-driven activity-based costing

      ○ Job costing
      ○ Process costing

Chapters 3 and 4

- How do we plan our costs and analyze the difference between actual and planned performance?
  ○ Standard costing
  ○ Budgetary control

Chapter 5

- What are the cost techniques that directly influence strategic decisions?
  ○ Break-even analysis
  ○ CVP analysis
  ○ Multiproduct analysis
  ○ Variable costing
  ○ Incremental analysis

Chapter 6

- What is the cost information required to manage our strategy?
  ○ Value chain analysis
  ○ Balanced scorecard
  ○ Cost reduction
  ○ Performance evaluation and improvement

Conclusions

This final chapter emphasizes the move away from "costing" past performance with only an internal landscape to techniques that are based on providing customer value, which is essential to success and even survival. This requires cost data that incorporates external forces and the future environment. And as our explanations demonstrate, the cost data and the formation and pursuit of strategy are intrinsically linked.

It is also evident that there is an overlap of some of the techniques we have discussed, or at least the sharing of common concepts. In a useful case study on lean accounting, the author notes that it is closely related to just-in-time and target costing and that it considers the entire life cycle of a product.[18] The move is toward increasing value for the customer and thus increasing value for the organization and toward a strategic cost analysis of external and future events.

The topics in this chapter are those that you are likely to encounter in large organizations and, in various forms, in some smaller companies, regardless of whether you work in the service sector, the manufacturing sector, or the public center. You may wish to refresh the contents of chapter 1 to appreciate how certain characteristics influence the system that a company selects.

We commenced this chapter by explaining value chain analysis and the balanced scorecard. These are both comprehensive techniques that embrace the entire organization and that analyze it in its environmental setting. Such techniques are not for the faint hearted. For companies to implement them takes substantial management effort and time, and requires organizational change. There are claimed benefits, but to achieve them 100% commitment is required at all levels in the organization.

The section on cost reduction offers a more practical and accessible array of techniques for companies, whatever their size. Although purists may argue that target costing, life-cycle costing, and activity-based management are not properly implemented by many companies, you need to ask yourself, "Does it work for me?" The whole purpose of strategic cost analysis is to assist you as a manager in planning, control, and decision making. If the methods you have implemented, however imperfectly, do this, you are to be congratulated.

The final section on performance evaluation and improvements builds on the foundations we introduced in earlier chapters. A consistent theme is the identification of cost information and appropriate measures that will encourage the performance you require and are capable of monitoring. Those measures must be selected by you within the context of the company for which you work and of the strategy you are pursuing. You are the manager: The use of cost information and strategic cost analysis will improve your performance as a manager.

As stated by Disraeli, a prime minister of England in the 19th century, "the most successful man in life is the man who has the best information."[19] Indeed, this is never truer than for today's manager strategizing in an ever-increasing dynamic and competitive global business environment.

Notes

Chapter 1

1. Juras and Peacock (2006).
2. Heller Baird and Gonzalaz-Wertz (2011).
3. Chenell (2003).
4. Fallan et al. (2010).
5. Blocher (2009).
6. Al-Hazmi (2010), p. 33.
7. Cadez (2007).
8. Cooper and Slagmulder (2003).
9. Porter (1985).
10. Sheehan and Foss (2009).
11. Juras and Peacock (2006), p. 34.
12. Scarlett (2007).
13. Portz and Lere (2010).
14. Hursman (2010).

Chapter 2

1. Compton and Brinker (2005), p. 16.
2. Elkington (1997).
3. Meeting and Harvey (1998).
4. Kaplan and Bruns (1987).
5. Vaughn and Nelson (2010).
6. Kaplan and Anderson (2004).
7. Rezaee (2005).
8. Modell (1996).
9. Tipgos and Crum (1982).
10. Dosch and Wilson (2010).

Chapter 3

1. Hussey (1999).
2. Libby and Lindsay (2010).
3. Pilkington and Crowther (2009).
4. Becwar and Armitage (1998).

Chapter 5

1. Calleja et al. (2006).
2. Macario (2006).
3. Kahneman and Tversky (1979).
4. Whyte (1986).
5. Adelmann (1983).

Chapter 6

1. Cooper and Slagmulder (1998).
2. Prahalad and Hamel (1990).
3. Al-Hazmi (2010).
4. Porter (1985).
5. McCunn (1998).
6. Lewy and Du Mee (1998).
7. Brierly et al. (2007).
8. Coyne et al. (2010).
9. Tanaka (1993).
10. Cooper and Slagmulder (1997).
11. Woodlock (2000).
12. Korpi and Ala-Risku (n.d.).
13. Convey (1991).
14. Miller (1992).
15. Turney (1992).
16. Powell (1995).
17. Powell (1995), p. 33.
18. Haskin (2010).
19. Disraeli (1880), p 156.

References

Adelman, R. L. (1983, October). The marginal contribution breakeven point. *The CPA Journal, 53*(10), 87. Retrieved November 8, 2010, from ABI/ INFORM Global. (Document ID: 212251886).

Al-Hazmi, M. H. (2010, November/December). Strategic choices: The case of management accounting system. *Journal of Applied Business Research, 26*(6), 33–45.

Becwar, G. E., & Armitage, J. L. (1998, Winter). Zero-base budgeting: Is it really dead? *Ohio CPA Journal, 48*(4), 52–54.

Blocher, E. (2009). Teaching cost management: A strategic emphasis. *Issues in Accounting Education, 24*(1), 1–12.

Brierley, J., Cowton, C., & Drury, C. (2007, September). The identification and type of costs used in cost reduction. *Journal of Cost Management, 21*(5), 34–39. Retrieved December 26, 2010, from ABI/INFORM Global (Document ID: 1373392001).

Cadez, S. (2007). A configuration form of fit in management accounting contingency theory: An empirical investigation. *The Business Review, 7*(2), 220–228.

Calleja, K., Steliaros, M., & Thomas, D. C. (2006). A note on cost stickiness: Some international comparisons. *Management Accounting Research, 17*(2), 127–140.

Chenell, R. H. (2003). Management control systems design within its organizational context: Findings from contingency-based research and directions for the future. *Accounting, Organizations and Society, 28*(2–3), 127–168.

Compton, J., & Brinker, T. M. (2005, September). How do we define cost? *Journal of Financial Service Professionals, 59*(5), 16–18.

Convey, S. (1991, November). Eliminating unproductive activities and processes. *CMA Magazine, 65*(9), 20–24.

Cooper, R., & Slagmulder, R. (1997). *Target costing and value engineering.* Portland, OR: Productivity Press.

Cooper, R., & Slagmulder, R. (1998). What is strategic cost management? *Management Accounting, 79*(7), 14–16.

Cooper, R., & Slagmulder, R. (2003, January/February). Strategic cost management: Expanding scope and boundaries. *Journal of Cost Management, 17*(1), 23–30.

Coyne, K. P., Coyne, S. T., & Coyne E. J. (2010, May). When you've got to cut costs—now. *Harvard Business Review, 88*(5), 74–82.

Disraeli, B. (2006). *Endymion.* Wildside Press LLC. Original work published 1880.

Dosch, J., & Wilson, J. (2010). Process costing and management accounting in today's business environment. *Strategic Finance, 92*(2), 37–43.

Elkington, J. (1997). *Cannibals with forks: The triple bottom line of 21st century business.* Oxford, UK: Capstone Publishing.

Fallan, L., Pettersen, I., & Stemsrudhagen, J. (2010). Multilevel framing: An alternative understanding of budget control in public enterprises. *Financial Accountability & Management, 26*(2), 190. Retrieved December 26, 2010, from ABI/INFORM Global (Document ID: 2048747931).

Haskin, D. (2010). Teaching special decisions in a lean accounting environment. *American Journal of Business Education, 3*(6), 91–96. Retrieved December 26, 2010, from ABI/INFORM Global (Document ID: 2064960331).

Heller Baird, C., & Gonzalez-Wertz, C. (2011). How top performers achieve customer-focused market leadership. *Strategy & Leadership, 39*(1), 16–23.

Hope, J., & Fraser, R. (2003). *Beyond budgeting: How managers can break free from the annual performance trap.* Boston, MA: Harvard Business School Press.

Hursman, A. (2010). Measure what matters: Seven strategies for selecting relevant key performance indicators. *Information Management, 20*(4), 24–28.

Hussey, R. (1999). A Dictionary of Accounting. Oxford, UK: Oxford University Press.

Juras, P., & Peacock, E. (2006, Fall). Applying strategic analysis concepts to capacity decisions. *Management Accounting Quarterly, 8*(1), 24–35.

Kahneman, D., & Tversky, A. (1979, March). Prospect theory: An analysis of decisions under risk. *Econometrica, 47*(2), 263–291.

Kaplan, R. S., & Anderson, S. R. (2004, November). Time-driven activity-based costing. *Harvard Business Review, 82*(11), 66–69.

Kaplan, R. S., & Bruns, W. (1987). *Accounting and management: A field study perspective.* Boston, MA: Harvard Business School Press.

Kaplan, R. S., & Norton, P. (1992, January/February). The balanced scorecard—measures that drive performance. *Harvard Business Review, 70*(1), 71–79.

Korpi, E., & Ala-Risku T. (n.d.). Life cycle costing: A review of published case studies. *Management Accounting Journal, 23*(3), 240–261.

Lenhardt, P. M., & Colton, S. D. (2003, May/June). The two faces of process improvement. *Journal of Cost Management, 17*(3), 46–48.

Lewy, C., & Du Mee, L. (1998, April). The ten commandments of balanced scorecard implementation. *Management Control and Accounting.*

Libby, T., & Lindsay, R. M. (2010). Beyond budgeting or budgeting reconsidered? A survey of North American budgeting practice. *Management Accounting Research, 21*(1), 56–67.

Macario, A. (2006). Are your hospital operating rooms "efficient"?: A scoring system with eight performance indicators. *Anesthesiology, 105*(2), 237–240.

McCunn, P. (1998). The balanced scorecard . . . the eleventh commandment. *Management Accounting, 76*(11), 34.

Meeting, D. T., & Harvey, R. O. (1998, December). Strategic cost accounting helps create a competitive edge. *Healthcare Financial Management, 52*(12), 42–51.

Miller, J. A. (1992, Winter). Designing and implementing a new cost management system. *Journal of Cost Management, 6*(1), 41–53.

Modell, Sven. (1996). Management accounting and control in services: Structural and behavioural perspectives. *International Journal of Service Industry Management, 7*(2), 57–80.

Pilkington, M., & Crowther, D. (2009, December). Minimal budgeting: The development of control mechanisms for small and micro e-businesses. *Research Executive Summaries Series, 5*(11), 1–6.

Porter, M. E. (1985). *Competitive advantage.* New York, NY: The Free Press.

Portz, K., & Lere, J. C. (2010, Spring). Cost center practices in Germany and the United States: Impact of country differences on managerial accounting practices. *American Journal of Business, 25*(1), 45–52.

Powell, T. C. (1995). Total quality management as competitive advantage: A review and empirical study. *Strategic Management Journal, 16*(1), 15–37.

Prahalad, C. K., & Hamel, G. (1990). The core competence of the corporation. *Harvard Business Review, 68*(3), 79–91.

Rezaee, Z. (2005). The relevance of managerial accounting concepts in the banking industry. *Journal of Performance Management, 18*(2), 3–14.

Scarlett, B. (2007, April). Management accounting: Performance evaluation. *Financial Management,* 41, 43. Retrieved December 26, 2010, from ABI/INFORM Global (Document ID: 1263956721).

Sheehan, N. T., & Foss, N. J. (2009). Exploring the roots of Porter's activity-based view. *Journal of Strategy and Management, 2*(3), 240–260.

Sims, A. (2001, September). A model approach: Generating strategic options. *CIMA Insider,* 24–26.

Tanaka, T. (1993, Spring). Target costing at Toyota. *Journal of Cost Management, 7*(1), 4–11.

Tipgos, M. A., & Crum, R. P. (1982, July). Applying management accounting concepts to the health care industry. *Management Accounting, 64*(1)37–48.

Turney, P. B. B. (1992, January). Activity-based management: ABM puts ABC information to work. *Management Accounting, 73*(7), 20–25.

Vaughn, P., Raab, C., & Nelson, K. B. (2010). The application of activity-based costing to a support kitchen in a Las Vegas casino. *International Journal of Contemporary Hospitality Management, 22*(7), 1033–1047.

Whyte, G. (1986). Escalating commitment to a course of action: A reinterpretation. *Academy of Management Review, 11*(2), 311–321.

Woodlock, P. (2000, March/April). Does it matter how targeted costs are achieved? *The Journal of Corporate Accounting & Finance, 11*(3), 43–52.

Index

Announcing the Business Expert Press Digital Library

Concise E-books Business Students
Need for Classroom and Research

This book can also be purchased in an e-book collection by your library as

- a one-time purchase,
- that is owned forever,
- allows for simultaneous readers,
- has no restrictions on printing,
- can be downloaded as PDFs from within the library community.

Our digital library collections are a great solution to beat the rising cost of textbooks. E-books can be loaded into their course management systems or onto students' e-book readers.

The **Business Expert Press** digital libraries are very affordable, with no obligation to buy in future years.

For more information, please visit **www.businessexpertpress.com/librarians**. To set up a trial in the United States, please contact **Sheri Dean** at sheri.dean@globalpress.com; for all other regions, contact **Nicole Lee** at nicole.lee@igroupnet.com.

OTHER TITLES IN OUR MANAGERIAL ACCOUNTING COLLECTION
Collection Editor: **Kenneth A. Merchant**, *University of Southern California*

Setting Performance Targets by Carolyn Stringer and Paul Shantapriyan

Revenue Management: A Path to Increased Profits by Ronald Huefner

Revenue Management for Service Organizations by Paul Rouse, William McGuire and Julie Harrison

Drivers of Successful Controllership: Activities, People, and Connecting With Management by Jürgen Weber and Pascal Nevries

Sustainability Reporting: Managing for Wealth and Corporate Health by Gwendolen B. White

Blind Spots, Biases and Other Pathologies in the Boardroom by Kenneth A. Merchant and Katharina Pick

Corporate Investment Decisions: Principles and Practice by Michael Pogue

Business Planning and Entrepreneurship: An Accounting Approach by Michael Kraten